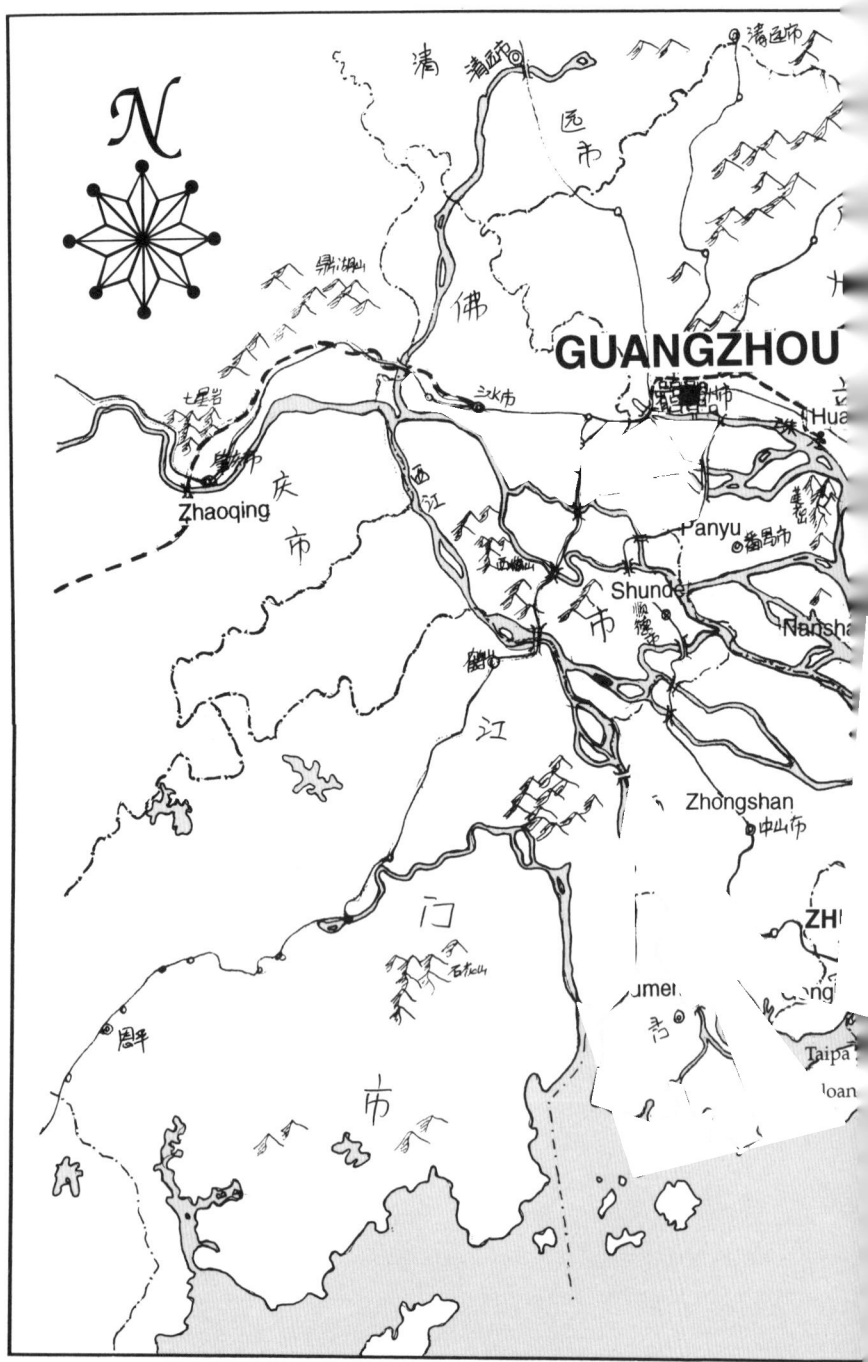

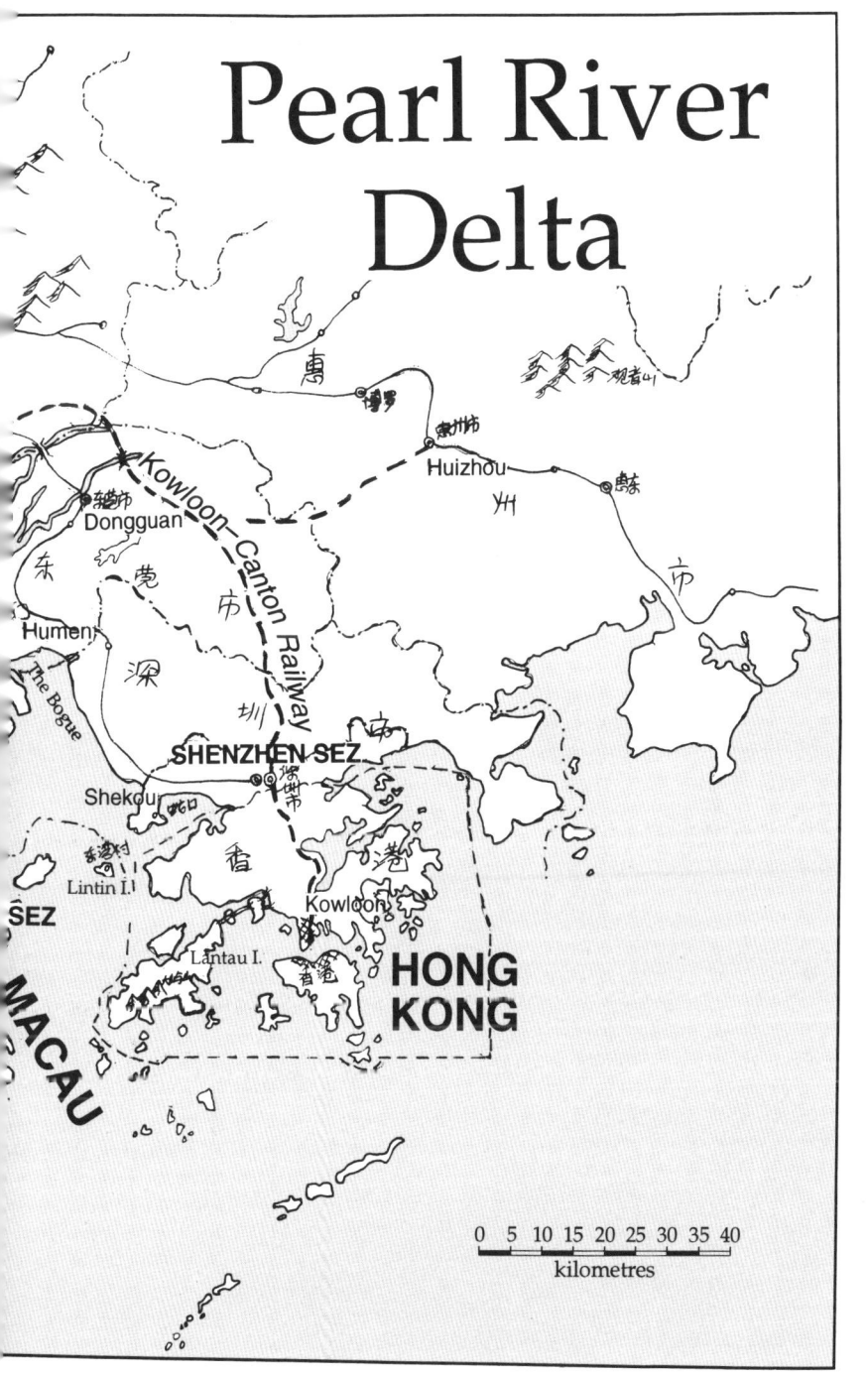

Hong Kong, Macau and the Muddy Pearl

Hong Kong, Macau and the Muddy Pearl

Travels in the Pearl River Delta

Annabel Jackson

Asia 2000 Limited
Hong Kong

© 1999 Annabel Jackson
All rights reserved

'Coffee-in-tea' is reproduced by kind permission of Leung Ping-kwan

ISBN 962-7160-66-0

Published by Asia 2000 Ltd
302 Seabird House,
22–28 Wyndham Street, Central,
Hong Kong

http://www.asia2000.com.hk/

Typeset with Ventura Publisher in Adobe Garamond by Asia 2000
Printed in Hong Kong by Regal Printing

First printing 1999

This book is sold subject to the condition that it shall not, by way of trade or otherwise, be lent, resold, hired out or otherwise circulated without the publisher's prior written consent in any form of binding or cover other than that in which it is published and without a similar condition including this condition being imposed on the subsequent purchaser.

ACKNOWLEDGEMENTS

Without naming all the people who have influenced this book, I sincerely thank those who allowed me to share in their personal Chinas.

Those who gave me not only their time but encouraged me to develop my own ideas; those who made introductions and travelled with me, and those I met by beautiful coincidence along the way.

Coffee-in-tea
by Leung Ping-kwan

Five different types of leaves brew a
Strong fragrant tea, in cotton bags or nylon stockings
Tenderly enclosed, blended. Steeped in boiling water,
Then poured into another pot. Differences in time elapsed
Affect the strength of the infusion. Can this balance
Be properly maintained? When the tea

Is poured into coffee, will the strong aroma in the cup
Overwhelm the newcomer? Or perhaps it can retain its own
Flavour: At roadside foodstalls, over the morning brew;
Accumulate street knowledge and worldly wisdom
A dash of daily gossip and good sense, diligence
And a touch of indolence. Indistinguishable tastes.

Translated by Leung Ping-kwan, John Minford and Annabel Jackson

Contents

Introduction 9

Chapter 1: Hong Kong 17
The Special Administrative Region discovers parts of itself it didn't know existed.

Chapter 2: Guangzhou 37
A look through Guangzhou's open doors to see whether the capital city of Guangdong Province has built on its historic dynamism.

Chapter 3: Macau 65
A 400-year-old colonial outpost struggling for modern relevance.

Chapter 4: The west side 87
Networking in Zhuhai, milk pudding in Shunde, modern lifestyles in Foshan and clean, clear air.

Chapter 5: The east side 113
Shenzhen, the wannabe Hong Kong, and its ugly feed-cities, and the girls who just want to get married.

Chapter 6: Zhaoqing, the scenic spot 125
The single tourist attraction in Guangzhou, where natural beauty is still more important than doing the next deal.

About the author 139

Illustrations

Pearl River Delta Map	endpapers
Village house, Guangdong	13
P K Leung, Hong Kong	24
Timothy Fok, Hong Kong	29
Star Ferry, Victoria Harbour, Hong Kong	34
Street restaurant, Guangzhou	47
Dancers, Guangzhou	49
Market, Guangzhou	56
Riverside, Guangzhou	61
A Galera, Hotel Lisboa, Macau	67
Espresso break, Macau	70
Henrique de Senna Fernandes, Macau	77
Ruins of St Paul's Church, Macau	81
Bridge, Zhuhai	89
Printer, Zhongshan	100
Shellfish, Zhuhai	103
Temple, Foshan	109
Downtown, Shenzhen	115
Star Lake, Zhaoqing	130
Rural road, Zhaoqing	135

Introduction

ONE EVENING IN THE MID-1980s in a small southern English town at a screening of Bernard Bertolucci's *The Last Emperor* in the local arts centre I ran into my family doctor. He asked me, as he has done every time he has seen me since I was the age of five, if my elder brother was still a lazy, good-for-nothing, or as he put it, 'still leaning on a five-bar gate'. Rather more interesting was his reply to my avowal that I had turned up for the movie as an enthusiastic consumer of film. His particular interest that night, Dr Dew told me, was to see a celluloid vision of the city from which he had just returned after a holiday-of-a-lifetime with his wife.

I seem to remember Dr Dew calling the city Peking — which is probably exactly how I, too, then referred to the place for I nurtured few Sino sensibilities in those days. I had seen Chen Kaige's *Yellow Earth,* on which now prominent mainland director Zhang Yimou was cinematographer, and had loved it, most particularly a folk song which I am sure was about onions; I had enjoyed equally the pursuit of the ultimate bowl of noodles in *Tampopo* from Japanese director Juzo Itami. But Madonna in *Desperately Seeking Susan* had also rather charmed me. Going into 'Communist' China was to me, then, something effected by other people like my doctor, or by missionaries. China was the sort of country, more alien than exotic to my mind, which I would never have the opportunity, or more honestly the spirit, to visit. At that time I was into going to New York and the South of France; I was also, simply, into living in London.

Early in 1989 an aeroplane on which I was unexpectedly seated landed in Hong Kong with me displaying what I still believe was an appropriate level of wonder at the spectacle of not only boats and buildings coming into finely-detailed focus but balls slipping into basketball nets and stray cats stretching out on rooftops under the afternoon sun. I stayed for a week to check the place out — and to get checked out. Everything, everyone, passed the test, and three months later I was living in the British Crown Colony of Hong Kong, which I quickly discovered was no longer referred to as a colony but as a territory.

Just enough time in Hong Kong had elapsed for me to ruin two very good pairs of shoes (I had little sartorial sense of how to manage myself in torrential rain), to find a quiet and calming but not too gentle walkway up The Peak and to discover that Cantonese restaurants were only as good as the person ordering the food, before I went to China. Or rather before China came to me.

It was Friday June 3, 1989, and it was raining, I think there was the threat of an early typhoon. Something was going on; young Chinese women in the office where I worked were in tears, that much I could understand. On Saturday June 4, 1989, and I am sure it was raining heavily again, those compelling pictures of tanks rolling past Tiananmen Square began to be broadcast to the world and to me on my brand new television set. As someone with a hitherto cursory British Empire kind of knowledge of Hong Kong, here I was getting a crash course in the relationship between reform and dogma in Beijing and in the relationship between Hong Kong and China; indeed in the relationship between Hong Kong Chinese and mainland Chinese. These events were to effect deep textural changes in Hong Kong society, changes which had gathered momentum after the signing of the Joint Declaration in 1984 between Margaret Thatcher and Deng Xiaoping governing the return of Hong Kong to mainland sovereignty, and which would quicken as 1997 approached.

Newly enlightened and crammer-educated in the deeper Hong Kong sensibilities which had hitherto masqueraded for me as a chauffeur-driven Rolls-Royce and chic little Chanel day suit, I can't say I rushed out to find myself a Cantonese teacher and took to Cantonese food with a renewed enthusiasm, or that I started hanging out in Hollywood Road antique stores specialising in Ming vases or Qing chairs. I didn't develop a sudden interest in getting north of the border to Shenzhen every Sunday. I was still negotiating ferries to Hong Kong's various outlying islands and trying to decide if I wanted to visit Macau at all. My only impression of the enclave thus far had

Introduction

been a dancing girl inset on the cover of a guide book to Hong Kong. The sheer drama caused in Hong Kong by the events in Tiananmen Square was, like it or not, the beginning of a deepening Oriental interest on my part to engage with the people and culture of the city in which I now lay at night my oft-times confused head.

The first trip I made out of Hong Kong was about two weeks after the tanks had rolled into Tiananmen Square. Having by now heard about the charming sides of Macau — colonial architecture and tax-free Portuguese wine — I headed in that direction and stayed in a mosquito-ridden room in the old, then faded green colonial Bela Vista hotel, ate Macanese shrimp curry and listened to the resident Filipino band perform a lovely rendition of *Masquerade*. I have subsequent to that trip written a book about Macau food and culture and spent large blocks of time living there.

Some months after that initial jetfoil trip to Macau came my first trip 'into' China, flying into the relative safety of the limestone outcrops of Guilin, a spot frequented by tourists. I later went to Beijing where I was completely overwhelmed by the magnificent scale of the city, and then suffered severe whip-lash following a traffic accident on the way back to the airport. I did the beautiful trip to Shanghai and Nanjing, Suzhou, Wuxi and Hangzhou to see the lakes and gardens and the famous, but to my mind ultimately disappointing, Bund. I had the misfortune to be in characterless Shenzhen for a two-day conference; and I went to Guangzhou and spent a relatively civilised weekend at the White Swan Hotel in the cause of research for a piece for Hong Kong's *Sunday Morning Post* as to whether Guangzhou might rival Macau as a weekend getaway. Most certainly not, was the conclusion.

It is quick and easy for Hong Kong residents to fly to Bali or Boracay to lie on the beach for a weekend, to visit the National Museum in Taipei and to tour Cambodia's extraordinary Cham temples. Large sections of the Hong Kong population thus question why any of their number would choose to go to China except for business.

Introduction

Shanghai with its vibrancy and Beijing with its splendour are two obvious exceptions to China-travel prejudice. But for most Hongkongers the experience of stepping over the border from Hong Kong and putting a foot in Guangdong Province, even if it does not render the trip as oppressive as going down a Dickensian mine, is analogous to the feeling of a British child going to Blackpool when her friends got to go to the Bahamas. Otherwise-independent Hong Kong Chinese women I know who travel freely on their own around the world refuse to go to China alone or even at all. Even travelling out-of-town to Macau for the weekend has more cachet than going to China, and sympathy usually greets anyone, bar the golfer, who is required to spend even a weekend in China.

These observations may sound superficial, but do accurately reflect how Hong Kong talks about China. The nature of the relationship between the two is in fact so complex and challenging that it is far more comfortable for most to ignore the realities, or make light of them. Or simply not to think about what lurks north of the border at all.

North of the Hong Kong border is a void which much of Hong Kong, in spite of the reunification of June 30, 1997, treats as a completely alien place. The level of ignorance of the region through all sections of society is extreme. Cantonese, with their intricate knowledge of food, might know about the famous dried orange peel of Xinhui and *lap cheong* from Dongguan City; certainly they'll know about the egg rolls and dried salt fish of Macau. But they are unlikely to know that the Opium War broke out in Humen, that Foshan has an important and traditional Chinese garden, or that Guangdong has a beautiful mountainous area in Zhaoqing.

Guangdong Province is simply not an area which most of Hong Kong can relate to. Reunification may be the politically correct word for post-handover realities, but what or whom is being 're'-unified is not immediately obvious, so bereft of indigenous culture were Hong Kong and Macau beyond the odd fishing village before European administrations took over.

Village house, Guangdong

Introduction

Before Hong Kong Island was ceded to the British in 1841, the area was home to 2,000 people; when Kowloon was added to the empire in 1860, a few hundred extra, slightly more established residents were added to the colony's population. The final expansion in 1898 added the agricultural hinterland of the 'New Territories'. The effects of this northerly expansion on everyday life were more widespread than the original cession of Hong Kong Island: one village in the north-east, Shataukok, was split neatly down the middle, half its inhabitants becoming British subjects with the remainder maintaining allegiance to the Qing emperors.

The Macau peninsula was granted to the Portuguese in 1557, two years after their arrival, but the construction of the A-Ma Temple a century earlier by a few Fujian fishermen marked them as the true 'founders' of Macau. Taipa and Coloane islands and their respective, isolated populations did not become part of Portuguese Macau until 1887.

In short, Hong Kong and Macau would never have risen to any kind of world prominence were it not for the requirements of British and Portuguese traders for bases in the South China Sea. Hong Kong today would probably still be that 'bare island with hardly a house on it', as British Foreign Secretary Lord Palmerston had it; and Macau simply an insignificant blob at the bottom of the western side of the Pearl River Delta, growing *choi sum* and fishing for shrimp.

Reunification is in any event a troubled concept. The German experience has put enormous strains on the people and the economy; the prospect of a reunification of Korea is even more difficult to envisage given the massive disparity in income and culture. Yet in the contemporary history of the Pearl River Delta, reunification for Hong Kong and Macau has been rendered more valid when viewed in relation to the development north of their borders of free market economics, to the development of Special Economic Zones (SEZs, four out of five of which are in Guangdong Province) and to a softening of the political position resulting in Beijing's espousal of an open-door policy and, more progressive still, a belief in the workability of Deng Xiaoping's 'one country, two systems' formula. Hong Kong has for years been preparing for increasing economic and social links with the mother country, spearheaded by the removal of factories to the mainland when labour costs in Hong Kong became prohibitively high. Fluency in the official language of China has grown dramatically in the past five years, with more and more jobs in Hong Kong requiring Mandarin skills in addition to fluency in English and, of course, in Cantonese.

There is little question that Guangzhou enjoys a tighter economic relationship with Hong Kong than it does with Beijing, but the city's relationship with Hong Kong also runs at a deeper level. The city, and indeed the entire province, displays a more profound cultural relationship with Hong Kong than it does with Beijing. After all, the majority of Hong Kong (and Macau) Chinese are immigrants, or the relatives and descendants of emigrants, from Guangdong Province. They share in their Cantonese-ness, and to be Cantonese is to be part of an extremely strong sub-culture within Greater China.

They also share an inter-linked past. The historical triangle of Hong Kong, Macau and Guangzhou was part of the main trading routes between China and Europe from as early as the sixteenth century; routes which diminished in importance as a result of a number of factors including the demise of the Portuguese colonies in Asia, the overall development of world trade which lessened the power of the Portuguese and, of course, the Opium Wars.

The triangle has undergone remarkable changes since. Hong Kong has developed into a leading financial market and a post-modern icon. Guangzhou has lost its position, formalised by the imperial government in 1685, as the single mainland city through which trade with the rest of the world could be effected. The city searches for a modern role. Macau has been transformed from one of the wealthiest entrepôts in the Far East — in its heyday and before the birth of Hong Kong, the enclave enjoyed exclusive trading links with Canton — to what some uncharitably but unfortunately fairly accurately refer to as 'the crime capital of Asia'.

The series of journeys planned for this book were intended to newly discover and newly define aspects of Guangdong Province captured within that historic — and contemporary — triangle drawn between Hong Kong, Macau and Guangzhou. Politics and economics naturally inform the text, but the journeys were undertaken first and foremost as personal, reflective journeys. According to the kind of people who need to label others, I am purported to be a cultural relativist. If that is true (hedonist I immediately admit to), such structure of mind may go some way to explaining why I seek during my travels to accommodate a range of opinions and positions. I am more interested in listening to what someone is saying and trying to understand why they say it, than stating my own case or imparting my own judgement.

If we're comparing the landscapes of Guangdong to those of Hangzhou or Guilin, Guangdong Province is not an attractive destination but it is an important destination. Travel throughout the delta becomes easier by the month with the introduction of new railway lines, road links, bus services and, of course, more and faster ferries.

Development of transportation follows development of intra-provincial business. By the mid-1980s the Special Economic Zones of Shenzhen north of Hong Kong and Zhuhai north of Macau generated the most business traffic, but as they have developed, so has industry moved to their furthest reaches, or to towns and cities outside the zones altogether. Guangdong Province officials in dozens of towns, seeing the success of such zones, have similarly sought to develop their economies through improving infrastructure and attracting foreign investment.

The journeys in this book are intended less to provide a travel guide to visitors, be they business people, willing or reluctant tourists, but more to explore in the light of reunification the cultural preoccupations and motivations of the inhabitants of the various cities, towns and villages along the legendary coastal waters of the Pearl River Delta. The starting point is always Hong Kong, in parallel undertaking its own personal journey to China.

Chapter 1: Hong Kong

LETTERS POSTED OVERSEAS and addressed to 'Hong Kong, China', the postmaster general of Hong Kong indicated, would likely be routed through Beijing and thus take longer to arrive than letters simply directed to 'Hong Kong'. Letters posted overseas, particularly in the United States and addressed to 'Hong Kong, Japan' would continue to make it as efficiently and smoothly to the territory as previously. So long as that 'C' word did not appear on the envelope. It seemed as if Deng Xiaoping's vision for a 'one country, two systems' really was going to work. Hong Kong wasn't really going to become part of China after all, at least that's what the post office seemed to be saying.

However subtle the changes for the operation of the post office, Hong Kong, the proverbial gateway to China for the leisure and business traveller alike, was a territory preparing to reach the conclusion of its own private journey. A journey which did not end on June 30, 1997, but which certainly began in the months leading up to the signing of the Joint Declaration in 1984; a journey which marks the return to the motherland following an acrimonious fostering out by China to Britain in 1841. Hong Kong's journey is one taken not by ferry boat, nor even by car or aeroplane. Yet it is a journey which informs all journeys taken to and from its shores by whatever means of transport or thought processes. It is a journey about politics and economics and power and vision, but it is also a metaphysical journey concerned fundamentally with Chinese-ness and, more specifically still, with Hong Kong-ness.

Standing on the top of one of the territory's rocky crags and looking out over Hong Kong, wondering what the place is all about, is a popular preoccupation, which with the arrival of 1997, became all the more pertinent amidst questions about what could change and what would change. What is it about Hong Kong people that makes them so successful in business? What is it about cities like Hong Kong that they prosper so? Surely there must be a formula? Was it necessary to answer such questions to know if Hong Kong could prosper post-handover?

There's a shocking sight in Hong Kong, one that jars even more painfully than the rubbish floating in the harbour, the fake Prada bag on a waitress's back or the OUT OF ORDER sign on the lift of the twenty-storey residential building when you're going to a dinner party on the 19th floor. That sight is the tourist who doesn't understand what kind of place he is visiting; a vision in dayglo orange shorts with a slightly-too-tight money belt around a sweaty midriff and a wilting Hong Kong Tourist Association map in hand. In London or New York no tourist would be seen dressed that way, but in Hong Kong, facing the shimmering sea, catching sight of a banana tree and experiencing the subtropical humidity, visitors imagine they're on an obscure beach in Indonesia and strip down to an entirely unsuitable wardrobe for Hong Kong. Unsuitable because Hong Kong is not a tourist destination in the conventional sense.

You don't go to Hong Kong to see things, things like temples and gardens and museums and lakes. What makes Hong Kong a fascinating destination is not traditional tourist traps, and let's be frank, there really aren't any. Those which do make it into regular guidebooks are, with the exception of shopping malls and markets, culturally unspecific imports which could be part of any city almost anywhere in the world. 'Southeast Asia's largest outdoor bronze Buddha' sitting newly-minted on Lantau Island is far less significant for the local population than Wong Tai Sin Temple in the heart of Kowloon where palms are read, fortunes told, and good luck prevailed upon. The Buddha could be sitting anywhere in Southeast Asia. Ocean Park offers a spectacular cable-car ride but the experience is less impressive than the trip to Singapore's Sentosa Island, and Ocean Park itself, a playground for water-babies, could be set up in Florida.

Anyone who tries to escape the summer heat, the all-year-round noise and the unrelenting pace of Hong Kong by heading for remote islands and fantasy worlds tries to escape Hong Kong itself. Hong

Chapter 1: Hong Kong

Kong is not for relaxing, sun-kissed holidays, it is for stimulating and challenging travel experience. There's plenty to experience in Hong Kong, too much for the senses really, but that's the point. You see Hong Kong but you also feel it; Hong Kong is a place you can feel so intensely you're almost seduced to believe you can touch it. You hear it intensely, in the shrill of the Filipino domestic helper community enjoying lunch and a game of cards together in Chater Garden on their day off on Sunday, in the incessant chatting over *yum cha* at the legendary Luk Yu Teahouse, or the perpetual buzzing of beepers and ringing of mobile phones wherever you are — even in the cinema, God forbid. You hear it on building sites where pile drivers exceed the approved decibel rating by more than two times. Even in the largest Cantonese restaurants, those with 200 and up seats, the noise level is above government-approval decibel ratings. And you hear Hong Kong's call to you personally, if you're interested to hear such a call.

The Hong Kong landmark not to miss is The Peak, not so much as a tourist attraction, particularly as the local population utilises the place so enthusiastically, but to provide clear insights into how Hong Kong works. You can be very un-Hong Kong and walk there, up a succession of roads, paths and steps though Pokfulam Country Park. The walk is not an escape from Hong Kong but a celebration of it, because at about the halfway point there's a glorious 200 degree view which stretches from the chimneys of Lamma Island right across to the eastern harbour and the old Kai Tak runway. Most people get to the top on wheels, and if that's not the bus or taxi kind, it should be the Peak Tram kind.

'One hundred years of accident-free operation' is indeed an impressive boast and the tram itself, a pair of shiny cars with slatted wooden seating, is an engineering feat. After the days of sedan chairs, the tram provided the major form of transport for top-ranking British expatriates who quickly designated this high point of Hong Kong as the coolest and thus most comfortable area for living, particularly through the hot, wet excesses of the summer months. Chinese were banished further down the hill to 'Mid-Levels' — the names themselves smack so beautifully of the British class system — though as Hong Kong prospered, so the Chinese began to acquire their own properties towards The Peak. Today the high-altitude community is a mix of dozens of nationalities and occupations, from diplomat to bank chairman, almost all of whom seem to keep a pedigreed dog, a currently fashionable Hong Kong status symbol, as well as someone to walk that dog.

The new tram station at the top opens out onto a dramatic fountain and a monument to shopping and eating — Hong Kong's favourite pastimes. Perhaps ironically in out-with-the-British 1997, a piece of modern London culture is likely to make a home here, in the shape of a Conran restaurant. A Sir Terence Conran restaurant; he who created the football-pitch sized Quaglino's behind London's Piccadilly and then, not content with making eating out in London fashionable again, bought the former cinema at Soho's legendary film industry address of 100 Wardour Street and turned it into the 700-seat Mezzo restaurant and bar. Hong Kong, for whom large dining rooms and a swell of noise around them constitute the perfect eating experience, will love him.

Around the top of The Peak winds a path for a walk which takes about forty minutes, though rarely providing occasion for quiet meditation. Most Hongkongers love noise and will frequently take a hissing radio along with them on a walk, particularly on a horse-racing day. Tour groups, families and school parties clog up the width of the pavement; it is a wonder that so many joggers can stand the stress of navigating so much dawdling. Later in the evening the pathway is far less populated, the silence disturbed only by the threatening growls of guard dogs and the whir of insistent mosquitoes. It is a great place to propose marriage over a bottle of Dom Perignon — at least that's what I assume a gentlemen was suggesting to the woman on the wall by his side recently. At various points around the walk, by day or night, The Peak becomes the ultimate viewing point for the incredible, architectural spectacle of a downtown which seems to know no bounds, now stretching beyond the original Central business district in all directions, including over the water to Tsimshatsui and, constructed on reclaimed land, its neighbour Tsimshatsui East.

Another thing tourists can do besides experience The Peak is mall hop, and for this they join a community of more than six million people which has collectively rendered shopping an art. People work hard, obsessively hard to much of the outside world, with their blurring of business and personal lives. But they earn more, often through completely ingenious ways — one shoe repair shop in Central had a notice in his window announcing HAPPY HOUR SHOE REPAIRS: HALF-PRICE BETWEEN 12–3PM — and they want to spend it. Shopping malls like the generously proportioned Pacific Place, Admiralty, is a Sunday afternoon destination in its own right, as well as a showcase for everything from Christian Dior and Dolce & Gabbana to Marks & Spencer and Muji. While tourists shop at Prince Edward and Stanley markets and hunt in tradesmen's lifts for the Donna Karan and Nicole Farhi factory outlets in the depths of Kowloon, locals head straight for the Lexus showroom or the prestigious and exclusive Landmark shopping mall in Central where they pout as they're pampered. And there's the eating.

Eating, when compared to shopping, may not look like an art but it, too, is highly developed in Hong Kong, even if the attitude to spending on food is rather different from the attitude to spending on consumer goods. Dressing well might require either a gold credit card or, in the absence of that, huge amounts of personal style. But eating well is not necessarily about cash. Business in Hong Kong is frequently conducted over a meal and, if appropriate, the host shows his respect for his guest through the huge amount he spends on shark's fin and abalone and the best French red wine. Eating the best that money can buy, however, may not mean eating in the fanciest restaurant. A restaurant does not have to look particularly clean or even boast a famous chef for gourmets to go there. No Hongkonger has a favourite restaurant. Instead, everyone has a favourite spot for congee, one for *dim sum*, another for shark's fin, for Shanghainese crab or for Chiuchow chicken.

A whole subsection of local eat-drink culture goes on inside the territory's five-star hotel restaurants, bars and ballrooms. Viewing Hong Kong Central from the Mandarin Oriental's top-floor Vong Bar over a glass of Bollinger without being disturbed by the horn of the Star Ferry, or gazing at both sides of the harbour from the corner suite at the Grand Hyatt Hotel in Wanchai with an exotic fruit bowl and without a bead of sweat appearing, may suggest a rather different Hong Kong to the one you smell on the street. But it is an equally valid if cushioned Hong Kong. Hotels in Hong Kong, some of the best in the urban world, reach their status not only due to respectable occupancy and at least two high seasons, but to the way those restaurants, bars and ballrooms are patronised by local residents. You could attend three cocktail parties a night, in their turn launching a new perfume, a new fund, or simply celebrating someone's birthday, and still not have got round everything you've been invited to. Some of the territory's top Western restaurants are still in the hotels — Grissini in the Grand Hyatt, Petrus in the Island Shangri-La — and the taking of afternoon tea in The Peninsula lobby or the Mandarin Oriental's Clipper Lounge is nothing less than an institution.

Not all Hong Kong is floored with marble and decked out in Armani. It is not all experienced shoppers, ladies who lunch, and successful young brokers doing million-dollar deals on the latest-edition Motorola mobile phone as they push through the crowds on Queen's Road during Central's mad lunch-time crush. Nor all crusty lawyers negotiating mergers for their clients over a pre-prandial gin and tonic at the frightfully staid Hong Kong Club. Riches-to-rags stories are told alongside rags-to-riches stories, artists struggle and, in a society offering little social welfare, the disabled and the disenfranchised are a reality. There are the humble, too: old men who do *tai chi* with the sunrise and walk their birds in Mongkok, tiny printers in Sheung Wan who keep their presses running twenty-four hours a day, hawkers selling fermented beancurd as offices begin to close. But they are merely the backdrop for the real activity of finding that business opportunity and closing on it.

Commentators have noted that this obsession with the accumulation of wealth occurs at the expense of quality of life. They ponder how people who are interested only in making money, who devote every waking minute to its pursuit, can be interesting in themselves or even to themselves. If culture is shared experience or a shared way of life, the cohesiveness in a society if you like, are we then to conclude that Hong Kong culture begins and ends with money? Superficially, this dollar-driven mentality can be attributed to a historical combination of smooth British administration and Chinese hard work; refugee culture meets colonial government with each side determined to separately make something from their unexpectedly mutual feeling of transience. Both sides were able to draw the same conclusion: If you weren't staying to put roots down, you may as well put away as much money as possible before you move on or back to Real Life. But there was a difference between the Chinese and the British. While the British confidently played out their well-practiced colonial role, with the sense of history and background and culture which went with it, there was no place, mental or physical, that the Chinese immigrants to Hong Kong could call their own.

'What is Hong Kong-ness?' was the question put to the floor by Indian-born Yudhisthtir Raj Isar, director of UNESCO's Culture and Development Coordination Office in Paris, at a workshop in Hong Kong in early 1997 about cultural development. The floor was silent. Dr P K Leung, poet, writer and then senior lecturer in the Comparative Literature Department at the University of Hong Kong, suggested that the silence itself already contained some important truths which could answer the question. He was not implying an absence of Hong Kong cultural identity, as some in the audience defensively assumed but, rather, alluding to the lack of dialogue and debate on the issue. The fact of living in Hong Kong has for years been one of the few recognised components of Hong Kong identity. It became a very important component. In few other cities do you find so many people talking so forcefully about their home, even if they live in a challenging, permanent state of at once loving and hating the place.

P K Leung, Hong Kong

Chapter 1: Hong Kong

Debate on cultural identity requires time, preferably in a quiet environment, both of which are so often a luxury in Hong Kong. To debate also requires motivation, and Dr Leung was not slow to point out that a discussion of Hong Kong identity can be a painful process, attended by a plethora of well-rehearsed self-defence mechanisms. 'Hong Kong culture is complex and perhaps contradictory,' offered Dr Stephen Sze, lecturer at Hong Kong's Lingnan College. 'We don't have a fixed or solid identity. But it is better not to be clear rather than to be fiercely nationalistic.' His reference to nationalism was an allusion to Middle Kingdom mentality; his reference to any lack of solidity pertained to the massacre in Tiananmen Square on June 4, 1989. He was setting Chinese-ness in opposition to Hong Kong-ness.

Dr Leung and I were later discussing the workshop over lunch at the University of Hong Kong restaurant. It was not a venue I expected him to suggest but we needed somewhere quiet where we could chat, which excluded anywhere Cantonese. We also knew we needed somewhere with a wine list and where the food was good to satisfy our mutual interests; we ended up with a table of competent Cantonese dishes except for an over-salted soup, and a surprisingly hearty bottle of Sicilian wine. These are my observations. Dr Leung did collude with me on the quality of the wine but he wasn't eating, he was concentrating so hard on the debate at hand. He introduced the issue as he sees it in this way: The 1980s, after the confirmation in 1984 of the return of Hong Kong to Chinese sovereignty, had largely been a positive time for Hong Kong–China relations, with Hong Kong Chinese finding themselves increasingly able to communicate with the new generation on the mainland. If Hong Kong Chinese, who had adopted that term for themselves after the Japanese occupation of the territory ended in 1945, might have been feeling increasingly happy with the Cantonese moniker again, the founding of the People's Republic of China in 1949 and four decades later, the events of June 1989, stopped them in their cultural tracks. Communication between the mainland and Hong Kong broke down formally and informally, with an estimated one in three Hong Kong Chinese taking to the streets to publicise their fear, their disappointment and, crucially, their search for a cohesive, shared identity. The strength of their emotional response at once reinforced their sense of Chinese-ness but also distanced them from the motherland. A new moniker was adopted: Hongkong-ese. It was the beginning of the politicisation of Hong Kong, a process which started well before Chris Patten arrived.

There was and is a strong sense that most Hongkongese do not want to, or are in any event unable to become simply Chinese again, at least they do not want to lose their emerging Hong Kong identity. In my experience, mainlanders are neither widely liked nor respected — 'northerners' or 'farmers' are often used as pejorative terms and certainly at blue-collar level a survey conducted in the territory in February 1997 concluded that Hongkongers believed mainlanders to be rude, dirty, ignorant people who persist in spitting and refuse to integrate. Interestingly, that is the view that many visitors to Hong Kong hold about Hongkongers. A Hongkonger rather higher up the scale told me he believed it will be easier for Asians of other nationalities working for his company in Hong Kong to do business on the mainland than it will for him, such is his suspicion of those north of the border. A feeling of unease runs both ways: mainlanders I have addressed the question of Hong Kong-ness to admire the Hongkongers for their hard work and responsibility towards their jobs, they recognise that they are very well off, but find them inaccessible and unfriendly. Layers of meaning float in answers like that.

A fact which will have to be increasingly faced across the whole Pearl River Delta region during the reunification process with Hong Kong and Macau is that there is no single Chinese culture. In a few identifiable ways cities on the Pearl River Delta are becoming united in a new urban culture, a uniform emulation of Hong Kong. Cantonese pop music from the territory, the Hong Kong form of spoken Cantonese, Hong Kong television and Hong Kong restaurants now provide a common currency across the delta. But the prevailing gap between the mainland and Hong Kong amounts to far more than colonialism, or to the fact that, while China became a communist state, Hong Kong was rapidly becoming one of the most open and

Chapter 1: Hong Kong

capitalist economies in the world. The period of post-colonialism in Hong Kong in relationship to a striking, Deng Xiaoping-instigated post-communist economic reform will not suddenly result in a warmly felt Chinese-ness among Hongkongers.

That colonial history should be allowed to inform debate about Hong Kong identity is not the mainstream view. The message propagated by the mainland is that colonial culture is negative and Dr Leung said he believed there is a real possibility that this attitude is being internalised by young Hong Kong people who subsequently shoulder some kind of guilt for being brought up under a colonial government. Colonialism is surely an undeniable part of Hong Kong identity and indeed Hong Kong's success, yet it is similarly undeniable that colonialism must take some responsibility for any lack of a sense of identity in Hong Kong. Dr Leung has been fighting colonial attitudes for ten years at the University of Hong Kong and can remember a classic case early on when a graduate student wished to take local culture as his research subject. The faculty deemed local culture as being unworthy of academic research. To compound the matter, in Chinese there is no clear distinction between 'high' and 'low' art, or between culture and Culture, distinctions much beloved in the West.

A painfully vague policy in the teaching of culture has followed in the wake of, on the one hand, closed minds on the part of teaching staff and, on the other, a British grammar school–style syllabus imposed on Hong Kong with scarcely any adaptation to local needs and interests. 'There is a lack of local context,' voiced exhibitions director of the Hong Kong Arts Centre, Oscar Ho, who has been involved in curriculum reform. 'It is not enough to look at Ming mountains and Michelangelo. We should be looking at an Anita Mui [a leading Cantonese pop singer from Hong Kong] CD cover.' Policies aimed to help the process of identity and integration after 1997 through a regaining or deepening of a Chinese — meaning mainland — identity, such as controversial moves in March 1997 to introduce the Cantonese dialect as the teaching medium in preference to the

English language in the majority of Hong Kong schools, miss the point.

Hong Kong is a post-modern iconic city though far less international, less the melting pot, less integrated than the fashionably dressed professional class, the smart shopping malls with stores selling every leading brand, the international hotels and the restaurants serving cuisines from all around the world might suggest. Walk into a little local tea-shop in Causeway Bay and you can order a drink called tea-coffee, a drink which Dr Leung has written a poem about. The drink is a blend of two apparently unblendable drinks; a recognition of things Western, in this case hot caffeinated beverages, accommodated in a quite unique way. Some analysts suggest Hong Kong, post-1997, might become more like Singapore, but the chances are that it will simply become more and more like itself through coming to know itself for the first time. The plans of the mainland may be a perpetual unknown and pertain to neo-imperialism, but at least Hong Kong will be freed from the rhetoric of the British Government, no longer the rope with which the Sino-British delegations play tug of war.

Timothy Fok politely punctuates his sentences with: 'Don't you think?' and says: 'That's another story,' nearly as often, at least he did in front of me. He was also keen to ascertain whether or not I was like the international journalists who come to see him with tedious regularity, their stories all but written even before they lay their tape recorders on the coffee table.

An easily recognisable face from the local social pages with his centre-parted hair, thick-framed spectacles and perhaps a Harris-tweed suit in mid-brown, Timothy Fok is one of the younger breed of businessmen who may not have the profiles of their fathers, the Henry Foks, the Li Ka-shings and the Y K Paos, but who nonetheless both define and are definers of the Hong Kong business environment today. Hong Kong rather than mainland born, bred in a privileged environment culminating in an overseas education and entering their own family companies, they have not been required to put in the

Timothy Fok, Hong Kong

incredible hard work, nor have they been able to match the mind-blowing successes of the older generation. Despite this, they're continuing in a tradition which could one day result in Hong Kong having families with international business interests on a par with the Rothschilds.

The Timothy Fok generation does not know China like the Henry Fok generation but extended-family ties to the mainland remain strong, and it is when you meet someone like Timothy Fok that you realise the depth of the relationship between Hong Kong and China. How central Hong Kong is to the development of China, how Hong Kong would never have risen to such lofty heights had it not been for immigrants from Guangdong. To meet blue-chip Hong Kong businessmen is to realise how key the drive of the individual has been, and continues to be, in the palpable success of Hong Kong. Businessmen like Henry Fok, already credited alongside Dr Stanley Ho with a leading role in creating modern-day Macau, play an even more important role in the increasing prosperity of the Pearl River Delta.

While almost all overseas Chinese, whether they're living in San Francisco, Sydney, Jakarta or Guam, send money back to their extended families on the mainland, Hong Kong businessmen like Henry Fok build expressways and universities and put in ferry services. 'People donate enormous amounts of money,' explained Timothy Fok. 'The West interprets this as favours or insurance but for us . . .' His voice trailed off as he looked for the right words. 'We are privileged,' he continued, 'we want to help people to equip themselves too. It is not about what you are doing as Chinese but where you are from. How good you are to your family is how you are judged. You are also good to where you come from. Roots are very strong, whatever passport you have. There is a glue which brings us together. A calling. And how can Hong Kong be useful to China?' he asked. 'By hooking up, not resisting. Our infrastructure is the only useful thing. Don't you think?'

Fok money and vision are behind the extraordinary rise of Nansha, close to Henry Fok's home town of Panyu, an inaccessible and thus poor town to the western side of the delta. Nansha, a deep-sea port which can take vessels of up to 50,000 tonnes, is already home to General Electric and also a Spanish bubble-gum company which supplies the whole of China with something to chew on. But besides its considerable industrial zone and residential area, Fok, who is president of the Guangdong Tennis Association as well as the Nansha Foreign Industry Association, has developed quality-of-life options such as a thirty-six-hole golf course on land which was a mountain. 'To build that in Scotland I would need an act of Parliament,' commented a bemused Irish employee. Fok also bought three million bricks which would have otherwise been dumped and built his own Tin Hau Temple which looks 1,000 years old. 'If you have an idea, you can get it built,' said Fok. He's talking about something which he knows he can give China and that is not really temples, but ideas.

Nansha is a port well known to Western colonialists, is referred to among British historians as the Port of Tigress, and it more or less represents the mid-point between Macau and Guangzhou at a stretch where the delta narrows down considerably. That the east and west banks of the Pearl River Delta are here at their closest point is a key reason for the Fok interest. Previously, the only way to get from one side of the delta to the other was by road via Guangzhou, with the single exception of today's catamaran link between the Special Economic Zones of Zhuhai and Shenzhen. It sounds obvious but it has taken a Hong Kong vision and Hong Kong resources to facilitate the necessary cooperation and synergy between the two sides of the delta for a ferry service. The concept of a single strategy to benefit two cities or ports is still a tough call in China. This ferry service now carries more than 15,000 vehicles each day. 'No one went to Macau for 400 years,' said Timothy Fok, 'until the jetfoil began. It is not a matter of how far but how convenient it is.' A thirty-minute road link, the Humen Bridge, is on the drawing board. People may talk about the reunification of the region since Hong Kong reverted in June 1997 and when Macau does in December 1999, but such a bridge would create a commercial and social unity in the Pearl River Delta region which was previously impossible to imagine.

Timothy Fok, Hong Kong legislative councillor with particular responsibility for sport and culture, was sitting on a very establishment pale-leather-upholstered chair in a meeting room in his company's offices on one of the highest floors in the Bank of China Tower, and was about to recount one of his 'stories'. This one would clarify his belief in the potential of a fully functioning relationship between Hong Kong and China. Henry Fok and Dr Stanley Ho were taking tea together in Macau, he explained, 'and this gentlemen with a very "characteristic" haircut and Mao jacket came over and started talking about tourism in China.' It was the days following the Cultural Revolution when tourism in China seemed to be the last thing on anyone's mind. This particular gentlemen with the haircut talked about the hot springs as one of the few spots in Guangdong which could attract people. Henry Fok gave the chap some money and wished him good luck. Within ten months a 250-room Chinese-style resort had been opened. National tourism was on its way.

If Henry Fok needed inspiration to look more closely at China for commercial ventures and the potential for international tourism, in addition to philanthropic projects, then this was clearly it. 'The problem obviously wasn't the Chinese,' — Timothy Fok smiled as he spoke — 'the problem was the system.' Timothy Fok's next story was about the construction of a golf course in Zhongshan. He personally felt golf was the way ahead for tourism in Guangdong. But the story was also about the ways he pioneered reforms to that 'system'. 'I knew nothing about golf,' he explained. 'Arnold Palmer was the only name I knew. I met him and asked him to design a golf course for me in China. He agreed.'

Timothy Fok sees the big picture. For him the future for tourism in China was not simply about bringing in foreign currency. It was about reform. At this time a cup of coffee costs the same in Outer Mongolia as in a coffee house in Guangzhou, he explained. He didn't let someone tell him how much he should charge for a cup of coffee. It was a question of supply and demand and of course if you were drinking your coffee in a tastefully-decorated, air-conditioned lounge, you would expect to pay something towards the chair you were sitting on. His company also introduced the first toll bridge in Guangdong, and now collects from over 3,000 toll lanes.

Timothy Fok's mind moves rapidly from one subject to the next, pausing only to reference an illustrated first-edition book put together during the Opium Wars, or to recall a quote from Singapore's Lee Kuan Yew. Next he was talking about the 1987 opening of the White Swan Hotel on Shamian Island in Guangzhou which attracted 40,000 local people. It was the first hotel which chose to welcome local people, and today does a remarkable *yum cha* trade every day and has become one of the most popular backdrops for family album snaps. It was also one of the first places to move beyond the dinner-at-six-or-not-at-all philosophy.

At this stage the only hotel in Guangzhou was the Dong Fang, really little more than a guest house providing bed and board. Timothy Fok, according to his philosophy that a hotel provides the first and perhaps most enduring impression of a city, saw the need for a place to stay which looked after the details. Riding on the success of the golf course in Zhongshan, he believed China 'could do it'. In local architects dampened by their experiences during the Cultural Revolution he found untapped energy, and when it came to training staff who had never even seen a hotel before, he called up Cornell University in America. 'I read in a book that you have a very good school,' he announced over the phone, 'but I am in China and I have 3,000 girls and boys who need the training of a very good school.' Cornell reacted promptly and booked flights; Timothy Fok remembers that the first lesson began with a piece of paper on which was drawn a very simple, smiling face. 'Ninety per cent of hotel service is about that,' said the teacher. It is a principle that remains part of the White Swan culture to this day, as anyone who has stayed at the hotel will attest. Timothy Fok's commitment to hiring local staff but giving them a top, international training has paid huge dividends. The White Swan has been voted Best Hotel in China and is one of the Leading Hotels in the World. 'It could only happen in Guangdong Province,' stressed Timothy Fok. 'Don't you think?'

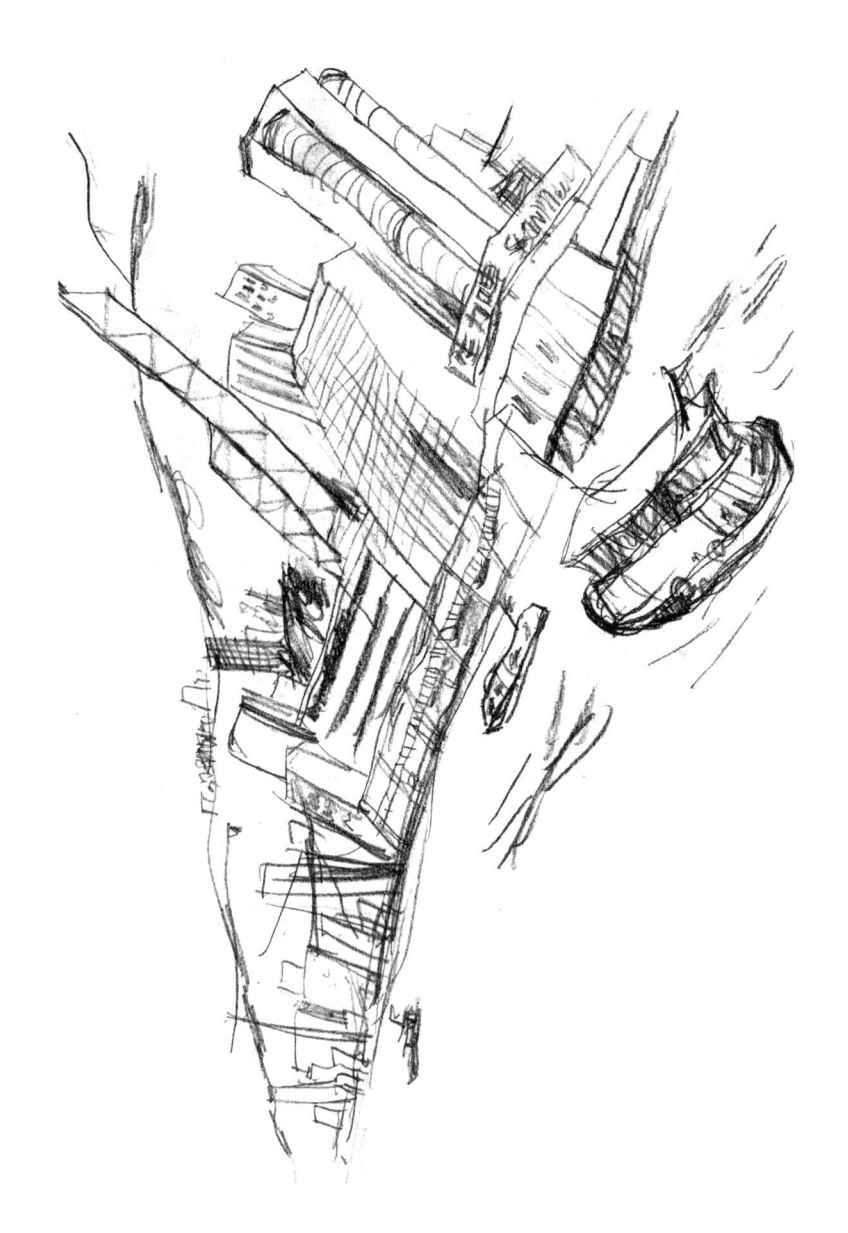

Star Ferry, Victoria Harbour, Hong Kong

Chapter 1: Hong Kong

Uproar in the press and a letter to the editor from Disgusted of Deep Water Bay. The Star Ferry wanted to raise the price for an upper deck fare to HK$2.20. Compared with any other way of traversing Victoria Harbour, that doesn't sound so bad, but it was only a few years back when at HK$1 the seven-minute journey from Hong Kong to Kowloon was often declared the most exciting and cheapest, not necessarily in that order, boat journey in the world. The new price still sounded modest but proportionally it was way above inflation and suddenly not only Hong Kong's affection for the Star Ferry but also the service's function as a blue-collar commuter route become clear once again. As recently as the 1960s street riots erupted at a previous attempt to raise Star Ferry prices.

The Star Ferry, one of Hong Kong's most exported images, is a very special, multi-purpose boat, and taking your place on one of its bi-directional wooden benches is one of the best ways to become enveloped in the magic of Hong Kong. On a night-time journey you become aware of the powers of man-made light which, when the sun has long gone down and the moon is obscured by a dense cloud, brings an unimaginable magical quality to the city. Lights reflected in the water, patterns of light in the uniform windows of vast residential towers, the crass but highly effective commercialism of the neon signs which cram every corner of every available building, the more purposefully-creative lights on major landmark hotels and office buildings; each flutter and flicker and play their indispensable part in making up the legendary Hong Kong skyline. By day the allure of the Star Ferry is scarcely less intense. You are out there in the very heart of the harbour as myriad other vessels fight for sea space — the ferry has the loudest horn, for sure — with views up from Central to the very heights of The Peak, and on the other side the Cultural Centre and clock tower spreading out to the old airport runway to the east and the massive Kwai Chung Container Port to the west.

Like almost everything else in Hong Kong, the Star Ferry works like clockwork, and it works for everyone. It is a don't-miss tourist attraction but it is also an endearingly efficient way to transport large numbers of people from one side of the shrinking harbour to the other. They are huge, heaving boats with user-friendly walkways on and off; that evocative shrill bell as the green light turns red, telling you that you've got about ten seconds to board or you'll find the gates shut before you.

Before the cross-harbour tunnel a ferry or rented walla-walla was the only way to get from Hong Kong to Kowloon. Today the Mass Transit Railway is the most efficient way to cross the harbour and clearly for that underground journey you may as well be under Tokyo as under Victoria Harbour for all you know about it. The journey from Central to Chek Lap Kok airport can be done in a comfortable thirty minutes, and then you're on your plane. Hong Kong forgets the importance that shipping and sea travel once were to it; that indeed it was shipping and sea travel which gave birth to Hong Kong and that they continue to generate wealth for many Hong Kong families. Today trips on the water, for most, are Sunday excursions to Lantau beaches and Lamma seafood restaurants, each journey made with hundreds of others on huge ferry boats. People barely seem to notice that they're on a boat. Ferries are as unfashionable to most minds as they are fascinating to the few, and most particularly those ferry boats which leave for China.

Chapter 2: Guangzhou

THERE'S SOMETHING POIGNANT about leaving Hong Kong on the night boat bound for Guangzhou. It's at once an event recalling the past and pointing to a definite future, a travel experience infused with history, politics, economics, philosophy. It is an extraordinary journey to take.

The night boat is a dusty, has-been vessel which smells of days gone by and surely represents them. Most people, after all, take the train. Journeys are almost always symbolic as well as experiences existing in real time and space. (You don't have to be a particularly sophisticated pop-song writer to know that travelling is not necessarily about moving). The sensation of taking the ferry on 20 February 1997, the day that Deng Xiaoping's death was announced and when just that morning 130 DAYS had wound its way across a friend's computer screen in a construct as in-your-face as the countdown clocks at Tiananmen Square and Shenzhen border control, was heartbreakingly intense. It was not a quick-fire journey in the direction of the would-be Hong Kong skylines of Shenzhen, Zhuhai or even Macau, but one to the historic, industrial, and very Chinese city of Guangzhou, seventy-six miles from Hong Kong.

What is most extraordinary is that people still take that night ferry, when the morning boat can deliver in three hours, and direct trains from Hung Hom in two-and-a-half hours. People used to take the boat from the south of England to the north of France but then the Channel Tunnel happened and boats between Britain and the Continent now seem positively passé, despite upgrading services in an attempt to draw back their customers. Who could possibly consider spending the whole night travelling from Hong Kong to Guangzhou? Even if the mental journey does take far longer. Price, rarely much of a factor in go-faster Hong Kong, is one consideration. You can get away with a little over HK$100 if you're prepared to sleep in a dorm and share a bathroom located somewhere at the other end of the dusty deck. That's half the price of the day-time boat or the train. Although paying for the top, deluxe cabin at the ticket office proved impossible for a non-budget traveller like myself ('one cabin, two persons' insisted the clerk every time I said 'one cabin, one person'), once you're on board there's the option to upgrade; a marvellous system which involves pressing your ticket onto a spike and waiting until the doors are heaved shut, then standing around the information counter for what seemed like an impossibly long time, waiting for someone to catch your eye. They must have their systems, you keep reassuring yourself, surely they're not ignoring me on purpose.

That little facility — and I'm so happy someone told me about it long before I boarded — resulted in an upgrade to that hitherto elusive one-person-one-cabin accommodation. You're now paying over HK$400 but, what would you know, the en-suite bathroom even boasts running water. The cabin door locks securely and the bed linen is clean. Sophisticated travel and accommodation demands were all of a sudden transformed into a simple desire for the basics. A friend had consoled me, as I stared dismally at the ticket in a Hong Kong bar, that I might end up sharing a cabin with Mr Right. I did hear once of a couple, now married, who met on a flight between London and New York — but on the boat between Hong Kong and Guangzhou? Well, someone could have met me, I suppose.

There's no need to dress for dinner on this boat. Leave the shiny accessories and Versace colour-combinations in the cabin — so as not to blend in too successfully with the mirrored columns or the red and yellow walls — and don't worry about spilling anything should the huge vessel suddenly hit a big wave. The carpet is red and brown and all those other colours approximating a diversity of stains. The dining room reeks of old ballrooms and drunken, unwelcome clenches or, rather less fancifully perhaps, of the past. It reeks of China; it does not reek of Hong Kong.

Besides spiking tickets, I had also got advice about how to eat and drink. More than one person, in fact, had said that the food on the night ferry is good, a comment which seemed hard to believe, but it is true. Not that length of menu or variety of dishes ever meant anything, but here both are extraordinary. That is lucky. Stuck on some kind of transport for any number of hours, the food and libations take on an important and distracting role. Why else would the competitive airline industry go to such efforts to plan scrutable wine lists and copious tasting notes, or leave such a long time between pre-dinner drinks and dinner?

On board are some of those strangely colonial Hong Kong dishes whose cultural or geographical origins may be clear but whose culinary execution are a strange hybrid: diced chicken with cashew nuts, curried beef or 'Germany's salt pig's hand' together with more traditional Cantonese fare like duck webs, steamed fish, braised eel hotpot, noodles and rice any style, and also beautifully simple dishes which Hong Kong rarely wastes its time with. Take eggplant casserole with salt fish. All that chopping of vegetables and barely anything meaty or fishy in the dish for which you can properly charge the customer and thereby pay whoever spent an entire afternoon chopping the vegetables. But you can find it on this boat. Or steamed beancurd with just a touch of minced meat and chili to give the illusion of the Sichuan *mapo doufu*. This is China, not Hong Kong, and the object here is to eat, not to dine.

Out on deck it was pure Hong Kong — for all to see. The doors closed at 9PM but the boat did not sail until 9:30PM — which left plenty of time for dinner before heading for the deck. No live jazz band or waiters mixing Singapore Slings appeared, but the wise travel with their own preferred bottle and preferred glass — more advice from a friend heeded — transforming the deck into the bar with the best view in the world. It felt so slow, so smooth, so gentle, as we moved from the shore — but who would want to leave Hong Kong, I wondered, as the vessel fought for water space out there in the harbour. The time-telling beams on Central Plaza in Wanchai, the stark lighting of I M Pei's Bank of China Tower in Central and the nearby post-modern (day or night) vision of the headquarters of Sir Norman Foster's Hongkong and Shanghai Bank receded, into focus coming the residential lights of the towers in Sheung Wan and round into Kennedy Town.

Chapter 2: Guangzhou

Distinctive aromas of wok-fried noodles emanated, still, from the kitchen, and the odd boat horn pierced the silence. For all the times I've taken boats across this harbour bound for Macau or one of Hong Kong's outlying islands, this time was different. I was not going to visit a friend on Lantau. The waters were the same, the destination was not. The boat was going to China, and that was that. Minutes out the sea traffic began to spread out, although the Kowloon side of the harbour was packed with moored boats. Planes were still landing every few minutes. As the industrial zone of the New Territories appeared, the Bank of China started to look like something made out of matchboxes. When you've stood below it and been seduced by its hard and powerful personality, or looked out from the viewing space on the forty-third floor and had an almost aerial view of Hongkong and Shanghai Bank and Government House with its surrounding gardens, it is hard to accept that the building could ever look like something from a children's play room. Hong Kong in its entirety was meanwhile taking on a character impossible to register as you rush along its streets on foot, and that was diminutiveness. Hong Kong is small, it is very small.

A slick Hongkonger out on deck on a mobile phone threw into the waters his empty San Miguel can (his preferred tin, clearly). The New Territories became China. Even the unsophisticated eye can tell when. That point when roads become poorly lit. When buildings look like they're built of slabs of concrete rather than bricks. When there's little sign of human life along the water. You never, it is said, step into the same river twice, yet to take the journey up the Pearl River Delta to Guangzhou is to take the journey of the British ships trading in tea, rhubarb, silk and, crucially, opium. Past Lintin Island, now inaccessible to the public but then the entrepôt of the opium trade. Past the narrowing spot thirty miles south of Whampoa through which all boats must pass, Bocca Tigris, or The Bogue; the Battle of the Bogue was one of the first times the British navy threatened China. Up to Whampoa (Huangpu), ten miles south of Canton and seventy miles north of Macau, which was the anchorage point for all

Chapter 2: Guangzhou

Western vessels at Canton. By the mid 19th-century, the area's docks and repair yards comprised the largest docking complex in East Asia.

To journey on a ferry is to partake in a travel experience involving a process we've all but alienated ourselves from. Even the British civil servants who left Hong Kong in March 1997, at the controversial price of some HK$60,000 per person on the last luxury liner, suffered a prolonged sense of loss as they left the territory. They may have known it was never to be a permanent home, but after in some cases thirty years' of service to the empire, leaving was extremely emotional. There were not-very-British tears in the eyes of respected territory figures. This is a facet of travel all but lost because of the aeroplane. Airborne transport presents it own challenges. The complete dislocation from time and space and any cultural or social familiarity which goes so far into self-definition, can force travellers to face the deepest questions about themselves. Where am I? Who am I? And indeed there are rarely answers except in the profoundest depths of self-consciousness. Anticipation and excitement may fuel the tourist; boredom or lap-top computers and regional business magazines may devour the corporate traveller. Most passengers drink a couple of glasses of Champagne, fall asleep, and avoid all the questions which surround traversing cultures and countries and the date line within hours. But travel is not trivial, and you certainly find that out on the ferry boat to China.

For anyone else besides me who is prepared to go a bit basic for a night, there's something almost time-saving about the trip if you think about it. Board around 8:30PM and have dinner, watch the world go by (or, in this case, watch the world disappear because leaving Hong Kong can feel like leaving civilisation altogether), and then retire for the night. The boat apparently docks by about 5:30AM but there's little noise until 7AM which is when most people wake up. At least 7AM is when I woke up, delighted that I had slept for a whole night, safely, and that the shower had mod cons like hot water. Whatever it is that happens at the dock between 5:30AM and 8AM is a mystery, but once the doors were finally heaved open, it was straight into a cab and you can catch an 8:30AM breakfast meeting (in my case an early check-in at the White Swan and a second, rather more substantial shower). In other words, you've wasted not one minute of a single office hour.

It was not until the queue to disembark formed that I realised quite how many people there are on the boat, and who. Groups of tough mainland Cantonese women with combed-back silver hair who have likely reached a great age but in that enviably resilient way can still get themselves and plenty of bags on and off the gangplanks. The odd Hong Kong businessman who has, presumably, been seduced by the ease of it all — plus, the mobile phone works for at least two hours out of Hong Kong. The odd quirky expatriate. The backpacker for whom a cheap ticket and a bed for the night are an unbeatable combination. Chinese New Year you have to book weeks in advance to make the trip up river, this mode of transport is so popular. After all, there is no baggage restriction and why not spend the money saved on extra gifts for mainland relatives?

If you thought Hong Kong harbour was polluted, its air thick with too many emissions, don't even let yourself look at the water quality here at Guangzhou's port, and wait until the sun has forced its way through until you take in the early morning light quality. It's dirty, it's ugly, but it's Guangzhou and this is a key city in that most incredible of world powers, the 1.2 billion-populated country of the People's Republic of China.

As recently as ten years ago Guangzhou, together with Beijing and Shanghai, were the only ports of entry for the tourist, and the southernmost city thus took a place on travel itineraries, albeit it a less important place. Guangzhou was still largely romanticised by tourists then as the site of the Opium Wars and the lavish lifestyles enjoyed by British and Portuguese traders both there and in Macau but it still afforded the excitement of 'going into China', as tourists used to describe the trip.

'If it was a Western group at the beginning of its China tour, we'd give them Cantonese food,' recalled the general manager of Guangzhou's impressive five-star China Hotel, Leon Lee, who has also worked in Beijing and Shanghai. 'If they were at the end of their stay in China, we'd give them Western food!' Today there are many gateway cities and Guangzhou is typically overlooked by tour groups, no longer a tourist destination as far as Lee is concerned. Guests at the hotel are either business people or overseas Chinese from Thailand, Hong Kong, Singapore and the Philippines, in Guangzhou purely to visit relatives.

Guangzhou's hoteliers have for years relied for good overall returns on the biannual trade fair. Running for more than thirty years but part of an international trading history of more than 2,000 years, it has traditionally been the ultimate showcase for every single product manufactured in China for export, keeping hotels full for up to a month at a time and in a position to charge extremely high rates. Lee knows people who have been coming for every one of those thirty years, but the fair is now losing out to specialised, regionalised fairs throughout China, and also to fax machines and courier services which have only recently reached acceptable levels of reliability. All this means most hotels run at capacity for only about four or five nights during each fair, and that even goes for hotels right across the street from the Guangzhou Trade Fair Centre including the China Hotel and its next-door-neighbour, the historic Dong Fang Hotel which before the China Hotel and White Swan were opened was the best of the few hotels available for foreign visitors.

Lee, who has been in Guangzhou for three years, predicted this erosion of business, and took out 200 rooms from his hotel, converting them into desirable apartments. At that time there was a city squeeze on medium to high rental apartments, so the highest priced were also the first to go. Then that market slumped — but Lee had predicted that too. He's now going into a new niche market which in his native USA is called 'residential inns' whereby serviced apartments can be rented by the month, the week, or even the day. Kitted out with six of everything in the dining room, ironing board, CD player and so on, someone will even deliver fish and vegetables to each apartment according to the individual guest's shopping list.

Lee is also noticing a slump in office accommodation, but he's confident that many Hong Kong companies will be moving their offices to Guangzhou, or converting existing offices to headquarters. He also believes the city's new airport, now under construction, will offer direct flights to major USA and European destinations and bring extra one-night business trade including pilots and flight attendants to hotels like his. Lee's other prediction is about the perception that everyone, including central government, seems to have eyes firmly set on Shanghai. 'After all, they're all from Shanghai,' said Lee, 'including Hong Kong's Tung Chee-hwa. But Guangzhou won't go quietly into the night. The Cantonese are very resilient, they're good business people.' Guangzhou is a tough city in which to run a business unless you can spot the trends. It is also, according to this expatriate, a tough city in which to live until you realise how easy it is to get to Hong Kong. The best thing about Guangzhou is that it is less than three hours from Hong Kong.

The latest trend to hit Guangzhou may be its most hard-hitting yet, for there are already compelling indications that, as mainland focus moves to Hong Kong, Guangzhou's days as the commercial hub of southern China are over. As Beijing becomes important only as the seat of power and diplomatic centre, Hong Kong and Shanghai become to Beijing what New York is to Washington. There is little question that Guangdong as a whole has an exciting and important role to play in the economic growth of the entire Asia-Pacific region, but the role for its sprawling capital city is unclear. Guangzhou continued to enhance its position as the eating and shopping capital of the province in the 1930s, but the development of the Special Economic Zones together with the unprecedented rise of Hong Kong during the 1980s have together made it difficult for Guangzhou to maintain its pre-eminence. The resources now required would be enormous to modernise this city with its entirely inefficient infrastructure, a largely dogged workforce which one commentator believes manages little more than three-and-half-days' work per week, and a considerable amount of historical baggage on its back. Formerly a port with special relationships with the West, Guangzhou was then crucial to China for doing business with the rest of the world. That is a role the city can no longer pretend to play.

Yet as the city hitherto at the heart of reform in Guangdong Province, the first province to introduce the 'open-door policy', Guangzhou has experienced great change, even as it has collected another layer of dust. What such reform has actually meant for everyday life may not be obvious to the casual observer. This reform cannot be measured in a Hong Kong-style Westernisation of culture because nothing so tangible has been able to occur. However hard the skylines of other mainland cities like Shenzhen and Shanghai might try to emulate Hong Kong's, the territory's unique character cannot simply be transported by doubling the number of Pizza Huts and bringing in Sir Norman Foster to do a building or two.

Guangzhou never tries to compete with Hong Kong, in any case, and strategists in both centres would prefer to see the two complementing rather than competing with each other. Hong Kong is close enough to be enjoyed by those in an employment or financial position to travel there as often as they like, with the result that Guangzhou is likely to become increasingly international but no more specifically Westernised in either spirit or culture than parts of Shanghai or Beijing. McDonald's may appeal to the children of Guangzhou but their parents don't enjoy burgers and the Hard Rock Cafe in the China Hotel remained almost empty even late on a Friday night. Outside upmarket hotels, retail outlets may be smart but they are more likely to stock local than international names or brands. With the notable exception of Sichuan food, it is hard to find restaurants serving anything but Cantonese food to any quality.

It is similarly difficult to ascertain from the physical infrastructure that Guangzhou is a city which has seen major reform. So the White Swan paints a marvellous picture on the river shore, at night wrapped in strings of tiny fairy lights to resemble a chocolate box. So across the formerly shabby and decaying forty-four-acre Shamian Island, the British and French concession from 1859, there are plenty of signs of life, and not just among foreign visitors staying variously at the Victory Hotel, the Youth Hostel or the White Swan. Restaurants spill out onto the street; there's even one called Lan Kwai Fong, named for the cobbled streets in Central where Hong Kong's hippest bars and restaurants are congregated. Smiling children dressed in primary colours run out of school to be met by grandma and a bag of buns; the soap shop and the shoe shop and the china shop all trade in very pretty consumables. In keeping with the traditions of Shamian, many of the consulates and quasi-government departments are housed there, now brightening up long-faded green and yellow facades with a thorough repainting. There are areas of new, coloured paving stones and recently introduced shiny seats; drains get unblocked and leaves get swept up.

But the strip of water which separates the island from downtown is still a stinking canal, while dark concrete overpasses are so densely constructed they put entire rows of shops in deepest, all-day shadow. Buildings layered with decades of dust and dirt, originally intended as stores or even offices and factories are now utilised as residences, and ill-considered overpasses are already clogging up with traffic. To driving madness can now be added congestion of the most polluting kind, and one can only hope that the city will be saved the construction of overpasses on top of overpasses by its new subway system, the first eighteen kilometres of which opened in October 1997. The ugly, existing overpasses give drivers a dislocating, voyeuristic view into first-floor windows. They pass close enough to scrutinise the cut of the jacket hanging out on the balcony.

We can talk about contemporary reform, but the fact is that Guangzhou has been an historic hotbed of political activity in opposition to Beijing, irrespective of the condition of its trunk roads. The 1911 revolution to overthrow the Manchus started from Dr Sun Yat Sen's home in a suburb of nearby Zhongshan City, and the Taiping Rebellion in the mid-19th century started just north of the city. Guangzhou rebels were the founders of the Communist Party, and both Mao Zedong and Zhou Enlai spent time there during the 1920s. Lingnan culture, born in Guangzhou and marginalised by the north, has profoundly influenced the development of modern painting, modern literature and even modern eating. Chinatowns the world

Street restaurant, Guangzhou

over are predominantly Cantonese, so keen have the Cantonese always been to travel overseas in search of not only money-making opportunities but adventure too. Beijing has always considered the Cantonese a dangerous lot over whom it can never maintain complete control. Crucially today the independence of the Cantonese manifests itself in the use of language. It is noticeable within the last five years that more and more Cantonese is spoken on the streets of Guangzhou — and not only on the streets. To the chagrin of other provinces, television channels and radio stations in Guangzhou broadcast in the colourful, expressive local dialect in preference to the official Mandarin. In politics, lifestyle or fine arts, all revolutions start in Guangzhou.

On the day of Deng Xiaoping's Memorial Service, a grey and muggy Tuesday, China shut down for two hours. Everyone in their place of work or study was obliged to watch the Beijing proceedings on the television. Students at the Guangdong Dance Academy in Guangzhou were required to stand for the two-hour broadcast and hang their heads in a show of grief. The students of classical and folk dance were, anyway. Meanwhile, in a newer building on the periphery of the grounds, members of the Guangdong Modern Dance Company, who train each day at the Academy, lounged around on chairs, chatting and smoking, considering among other things the economics of shutting down an entire country for two hours.

The implications of such contrasts in style are clear. Political reform and economic development bring in their wake creative and independent thought; indeed they cannot be successfully instigated without the appropriation of a new mind-set. And this new freedom to engage in personal expression rather than ritual and rhetoric is precisely what is being practiced in the ground-breaking Guangzhou dance company. According to Willy Tsao, founder and artistic director of Hong Kong's City Contemporary Dance Company, one of Hong Kong's most powerful voices on dance, and now artistic director and patron of the Guangdong Modern Dance Company, it could only happen in Guangzhou.

Dancers, Guangzhou

Willy and I were drinking Chinese tea from plastic cups and eating a breakfast of fried noodles and a congee flavoured with 1,000-year-old egg from polystyrene bowls in the buffet car of the train which runs on the Kowloon–Canton Railway, on our way to Guangzhou to watch a couple of dance workshops. He was telling me about his apartment in Guangzhou and how good the city is for him artistically — if only because there are so few Hong Kong-style distractions. Back in harshly paced Hong Kong, as a spokesman for and within the dance community, he sits on committees and goes from meeting to meeting. Personally it has been good for him to divide his life between Hong Kong and Guangzhou; professionally the company could never have evolved as it has, had it not been established in Guangzhou. Developing modern dance here in this southernmost city rather than under the over-attentive eyes of Beijing or even Shanghai has been and remains vital to the success of the company. Media scepticism about the ability of Guangzhou, a so-called cultural desert, to produce something artistically interesting, has kept international exposure at usefully low levels, again benefiting the quiet development of the company away from the world spotlight.

The exciting work coming out of the company should also show, said Willy, that he had no fears, as a modern dance professional, about Hong Kong's return to mainland sovereignty, or of any potential dilution of the Hong Kong artiste's freedom to express. He's seen what can happen in Guangzhou, so why should Hong Kong, particularly in the light of its Western and democratically influenced backdrop, believe it will be driven to artistic compromise after the change of sovereignty? Not everyone would agree, but those who choose to disagree with him should be able to understand how Willy can make that kind of statement in the specific context of dance.

The company with its sixteen dancers from eight provinces was the vision of an elegant and dynamic, though not typically dancer-shaped, Shanghainese woman called Yang Meiqi who, after training from the age of eleven at the Beijing Dance Academy in Chinese National Dance Drama and developing a career as a dance teacher, was named head of the 700 student-strong Guangzhou Dance

Academy in 1986. On the proceeds of a grant from the Asian Cultural Council, she went to the USA that same year to observe dance development in New York and to participate in the American Dance Festival. At the back of her mind the question was already being formulated, of how she could break her own students out of following the classic, traditional mould and encourage more creativity. In modern dance she found the creative form she had been searching for. 'Modern dance is an art form based on the individual person,' said Madam Yang, using her flexible body to illustrate her point.

I met Madam Yang first about five years ago when the company danced its inaugural performance at Guangzhou's Friendship Theatre and her intellectual rigour first impressed me then. She turns a question into a discursive point and never answers without establishing a context for her comments. 'What a choreographer does is an expression of his personality,' she continued between phone calls in her office above one of the company's rehearsal rooms. An agreement was reached whereby teachers would be supplied by the American Dance Festival and other European sources for four years, so Madam Yang decided to establish a modern dance class at her Academy. She scoured the provinces of China for classical and folk dancers she believed could be transformed from physically beautiful performers with minds focused on developing the potential of their bodies into world-class artistes with a desire to express the beauty of their minds through their exceptional bodies.

Government officials were fundamentally suspicious of this thoroughly Western art form and its potentially subversive elements, but pragmatic concerns were also raised, such as whether there would be any audience for modern dance. Madam Yang was given three years to establish an 'experimental' company, a word which still makes part of the company's Chinese name though it was dropped from the English title. Today, she said, the only overt limits to freedom of expression are those faced by most companies in most countries in the world: holding back from biting the hand that feeds — the company is, after all, government-funded — and, by law, not presenting obscenity on stage. The latter would not, in any case, be acceptable to the local audience, said Madam Yang. There is still a sense in which the company must be careful about its performances at home, still a sense in which it must cater to the broad public, though it is gradually building and educating an appreciative dedicated audience. A rehearsal studio has been converted into a 100-seat theatre for intimate performances, to provide a regular diet of dance for those particularly interested, as well as to give the dancers the maximum opportunity to perform. This theatre is another reason to be in Guangzhou, Willy said: a venue which amounts to a private theatre would never have been allowed in Beijing. The local audience beyond the four walls of this dedicated theatre remains noisy, trained from a young age by their experience of attending Cantonese Opera performances in which food and drink are a key element to the enjoyment of the day, and during which audience members get up and down at will, remaining quiet only during their favourite bits. Within the four walls of this private theatre, in a luxury for the dancers, all is quiet.

Government attitudes to the practice of a modern, Western art form in China have now completely changed. It was when individual dancers began to win firsts, seconds and thirds in international competitions in cities as influential in the modern dance world as Paris and New York that the government began to soften its approach to the Guangdong company. Suddenly modern dance was being perceived as a complement to the classic and folk traditions, seen as an altogether positive symbol of what the 'open-door policy' could achieve. 'Now China is part of the modern world we should have some modern arts and this company can represent such arts,' an official from the Chinese Embassy apparently said after a performance by the company in Germany.

The company's first set of dancers, sharing a pull to the West, have now all left except for one (he is a teacher in the company), some to pursue dance careers abroad, some to change careers, some to marry and have children. The current group of dancers, although they love their annual overseas tours and welcome the personal development which comes from such travel opportunities, are extremely happy to be with the Guangdong company and radiate the new sensibility of dance nationalism. They know they are good together, they know they are special, and they know they are involved in something very exciting. This is not modern dance per se, not a copy of a Western form, but the emerging essence of Chinese modern dance. This knowledge leaves them fetchingly unselfconscious. 'It is not about pride as such,' said Sang Jijia, expressing his feeling about dancing with the company. Sang Jijia is a tremendously tall Tibetan dancer with a mane of thick hair which he wears in a braid down his back, and a physical beauty Hollywood would go gaga over. He listened shyly to an introduction of himself as Tibet's ground-breaking, first modern dancer. 'This is just where I work,' he shrugged. That the company members are far less precious about their bodies than Western dancers is immediately obvious. They don't have pronounced muscles (of course some of their training is different from that in the West) and they look lean rather than thin. They eat what they want when they want, and plenty of them smoke cigarettes and drink beer. 'We think about ourselves as people first, dancers second,' offered one dancer.

The morning I travelled up to Guangzhou with Willy the company received a visit from the Richard Alston Dance Company, touring China from London on a British Council–funded tour. The two companies showed each other their work. The British dancers were cool and detached, emotional depth powerfully present but submerged beneath the measured surface. Among the Chinese dancers, the energy and emotion were far more explicit. Richard Alston and Willy spoke a common language of floor training and release therapy, of Martha Graham and Merce Cunningham, but it was clear as the dancers from both companies combined for a workshop that modern dance in China is already developing its own distinct voice. 'Personality is influenced by cultural background,' expounded Madam Yang, 'so of course there are some very special, unique things about Chinese modern dance.' For Xing Liang, a tall and lean dancer from Beijing with close-cropped hair who was wearing a City Contemporary Dance Company sweatshirt given to him during a visit to Hong Kong: 'Western modern dance inspires me in terms of structure, but Chinese modern dance comes from inside so the philosophy is different.' Teaching himself philosophy by reading a range of great thinkers in his spare time, he explained: 'I used to think about how to dance, how to make a movement. Now my question is: Why to dance at all? I used to want to make new movement, now I want to find movement to express exactly what I want to express.'

True, the dancers still have to work within a set of government-issued guidelines, I was told by Willy rather than by Madam Yang, and in this they are no different to the swell of privately owned businesses flourishing in the Pearl River Delta. But the experience of learning to function effectively even within apparent constraints is also a skill shared between artists and businessmen. 'Art is still essentially seen as propaganda in China,' said Willy. 'We still have to do work each year for the government. We have to follow what is called "the main melody". That means we have to emphasise ethnic Chinese culture; the traditions and values of China. That is what we're doing in this period. It could be that in the next period the main melody will be different. But right now the value of art is judged by how much you are in harmony with this main melody.' That those given the task of making those judgements have scant knowledge of dance and miss all subtlety works beautifully in the company's favour.

Willy is one of a growing number of Hong Kong Chinese who is not only talking about new challenges and opportunities for artistic cultivation after the handover. As an artist, working in China is affording inspiration which Hong Kong or the West fails to deliver. 'I am so grateful for the way China has opened up my mind. I am no longer wondering what to do next in my work.' He talks of the politicisation of Hong Kong, and how the territory has been playing the same tune since 1984 when change of sovereignty was confirmed. But the territory has failed to get beyond, as Willy sees it, issues of identity. The search in 1984, when Hong Kong residents started to seriously question who they were and what they were, was repeated in 1989 after the Tiananmen incident ('incident' being the currently politically correct way to describe the events of June 4). During the 1990s, as the year 1997 loomed, the questions remained the same. Once 1997 arrived, Willy admits to having been entirely bored by the continual press coverage of the smallest possible issues relating to the handover.

A Chinese proverb suggests that the perfect way to manage one's life, should one be able to assume such control, is to be born in Suzhou, to live in Hangzhou, to eat in Guangzhou and to die in Liuzhou. Suzhou, home to architect I M Pei whose family home and garden can still be visited, is a delightful city from where the most beautiful women in China are said to come — although young Chinese men say such women are unfortunately long gone, bound for the bright lights and bulging wallets of cities like Zhuhai. Hangzhou, with its romantic lake-side setting and mountains apparently offers a perfect environment in which to live, and that could still be true. Liuzhou is still famous for wood, excellent for making coffins. But is the best food still to be had in Guangzhou? Probably Hong Kong long eclipsed the city in this regard, and though nearby Shunde is famous beyond Guangzhou for the variety of its agriculture, for cultivating the province's best chefs, and for creating several unique dishes, there are few restaurants of interest in Shunde in spite of its show of prosperity.

A riddle, a riddle rather than proverb, which is very popular in the north of China, is all about what the Cantonese will eat. Anything that's got legs and is not a table. Anything that has wings and is not an aeroplane. What is beyond question is the fact that you can see in Guangzhou more of what the Cantonese like to eat — before it reaches the table — than in any other city in Guangdong. Certainly more than you can see in Hong Kong where many foods have now been declared protected species, or even in the rather more liberal Macau where those with the right connections can apparently still order monkey brains. In Guangzhou, a city frequented by businessmen and often reluctant tourists, and one with few specific tourist attractions besides the odd park and the odd temple, a bizarre attraction has grown up around Qing Ping market.

Covering several dingy blocks over the bridge from Shamian island, Qing Ping is a maze of lanes lined with stalls and little shops, interspersed with quiet residential lanes where old women sit and

Market, Guangzhou

watch the world go by, where children play with a ball, and where tailors do their alterations on a table just outside someone else's front door. Qing Ping is the place to buy water spinach and coriander, oranges and pomelos, dried salted fish and dried mango strips. But what the tourist, and in particular the Western tourist goes to see, is not the fruit nor even exotic medicinal preparations like black rubbery deer's penis or dried bat wings. They go to see the white kittens and snarling civet cats in cramped cages, the badgers with legs bleeding from injuries sustained in the trap they were caught in; to see bear paws, huge turtles, scorpions and poisonous snakes.

The atmosphere in the market is cold and unfriendly, with stall-holders crouched on their haunches above their stalls, watching the throng passing through, or perhaps chopping meat into different cuts, or spiking snakes onto nails. A little crowd often gathers around the plastic baths of scorpions, and rabbits sit freely on the top of bamboo baskets nibbling on leaves and looking lively. Otherwise there's very little happening, in great contrast to the wholesale fish market some five minutes away. Operating at night under the harsh glare of fluorescent lighting, the fish market is a hive of frenetic activity, a haven of fun and smiles and laughter. You feel a love of food and not a hint of defensiveness or suspicion which is far more a product of the Qing Ping crowd. Should a visitor move to take a photograph of a beaver or a dog, stall-holders are likely to erupt in panic. Here at the fish market they encourage as much interaction as possible. Along certain of the fish market's lanes, stalls sit side-by-side with restaurants, the managers of which boast day-to-day knowledge of what is in season and what arrived just minutes ago, as well as which rare delicacies are available that very night. Lorries come and go to both deliver and collect fish, and everyone wears tough rubber gloves and sloshes around in Wellington boots. The uneven paving stones on the ground are littered with rubbish but the ground is washed down regularly, and the water in the fish and seafood tanks is spotlessly clean. A fresh water supply is crucial to such an operation and in Guangdong such a supply is no longer a problem.

You can find any kind of fish or seafood you want. There are the popular Cantonese white-flesh fish of every size, prawns and shrimps in every variety, eel, mussels and clams, but there are also more exotic looking fish and delicacies like sea urchins with their hedgehog shells, beautiful for eating raw as the Japanese do in the form of *uni sushi*. The sight of this *gwaipor* (foreign devil, female) asking to have a sea urchin cut open there and then encouraged a crowd to gather around. The staff did not know how to open that shell expertly, so it remained for the owner to wander over and extract sections of orange-coloured, mango-textured flesh from the shell and deposit them in a little white plastic spoon for tasting. The crowd was probably waiting for a look of disgust to appear on my face; when I smiled appreciatively, it was as if cheers broke out. Eat what the Cantonese like to eat and you're accepted; it is a rule which extends across other cultures too: when in Rome. . . .

Qing Ping remains more famous than the night fish market, so travellers find their way to that rather surly day market. For most visitors the reaction is less an interest or even incredulity that someone would want to go to the bother of eating a skin-and-bones kitten or a chicken foot or a tiny quail, and more often the launching into a tirade about endangered species or a lapse into sentimentality about kittens while they spare no thought for a rice bird or wild boar. Indeed, as more Hong Kong Chinese take cats and dogs as pets, they too cry out in shock at the sight of dead animals in cages with live animals by their side. But ask someone in Guangzhou why they like to eat such animals and they will reply that actually they don't eat such things, that's what everyone else does. Or they will simply fail to understand the question; fail to understand why eating such a delicacy as owl, if you are lucky enough to be able to afford it, should be anything exceptional.

Eating everything you can find might be about survival at some specific historic times, and Guangzhou has experienced food shortages as recently as the early-1970s. But in a culture which loves to eat, the broad-based notion of what constitutes food is surely about pushing back the boundaries of what is acceptable to eat, creating almost daily new dishes with new exotic ingredients, bringing a sense of excitement, adventure and anticipation to the family dinner table.

For all the subtle differences in culture from city to city within the Pearl River Delta and wider Guangdong Province, the love of eating is a constant. Where most cultures would say they eat to live, the Cantonese say they live to eat. Eating in Guangdong, more than any other place in China, is a joyous, social occasion, entirely informal, with Italian home cooking and dining its only point of reference. The mess and the noise in a Chinese restaurant are unmistakable, reaching their peak in Hong Kong, and that's all part of the informality. Children are taught little in the way of table manners but they are told to keep both hands visible during meal-times; even that 'rule' has gone by the time you're old enough to answer back. Children are also rebuked for holding their chopsticks in their left hand, but today that predilection carries far less stigma. Although almost all non-Chinese find it hard to do, it is considered among Chinese more polite to pick up a rice bowl and shovel its contents into the mouth than to leave the bowl stationary on the table, a position which makes it more difficult to eat the rice, in any event. Visitors who might worry about which spoon to use or whether to use a spoon at all, whether to set their bowl on the plate or straight onto the table, whether to eat direct from their bowl of rice or deposit rice from that bowl into the bowl in front of them need not worry. A quick look around the table reveals that every variation on every theme will be effected. Any kind of appreciative slurping noise, crunching noise, sucking noise, or burping at the table, is also entirely acceptable.

Even if today young people are losing cooking skills through lack of interest or time, particularly in the resurgence of a high-standard restaurant scene in Guangzhou, there's usually one older member of the extended family who still loves to cook and can do so beautifully. Families gather together every evening to eat together. Friends who run into each other on the street immediately suggest they go to eat together. Greetings like 'hello' translate literally from the Cantonese as 'have you eaten rice yet'. The Cantonese also know an enormous amount about food. Ordering can take a considerable time, charged with discussions with waiting staff about what is good, what is special, and how something will be cooked. Such deliberations do not always translate as good food — knowing about dishes in theory and knowing what is good food and thus what is a good restaurant are not necessarily two sides of the same coin, unfortunately — but the process is always intense and very involving.

The lunch-time boat bound for Hong Kong is scheduled daily for one in the afternoon and leaves from the same godforsaken pier into which the night ferry from Hong Kong lumbers. Even the best-intentioned taxi driver, who could surely locate the new train station without hesitation, has a problem finding this almost abandoned pier. At nine in the morning as passengers arrive through passport control, a few friends and family members wait to greet the arrivals and a couple of taxi drivers wait optimistically for a fare, surprised and delighted when they get one. There are no roadways, just strips of tarmac and rows of tumbledown cottages; arriving here is like landing at a little fishing village, not one of China's largest cities. Nothing appears to have changed here for thirty years, and that includes staff uniforms which still feature a red band worn above the elbow of the left arm. Getting out of this little area involves traversing a maze where cars driving in opposite directions share a single lane and where no amount of honking of horns will hurry along elderly pedestrians or younger cyclists. Once the last passenger from Hong Kong has disappeared, nothing whatsoever happens for the next three hours.

Passengers on the lunch-time boat are requested on the ticket to embark one hour before sailing. What in fact happened one hour before sailing was that someone took out a plastic bag containing tickets for sale and wads of Hong Kong dollars, for this is a legal money-changing point; someone wandered over to buy a ticket and secure some Hong Kong dollars. A gate or two got closed, a ticket or two got checked, a friend or two said their farewells. Empty rice bowls were rinsed out, and idling members of staff thus far lounging around on a pair of old leather-look sofas strolled around instead of just sitting still. The cavernous departure hall smelt of toilets and raw meat —

Riverside, Guangzhou

and is exactly the kind of place where you neither partake of food nor visit a washroom. The hall's walls were lined with faded lime green chairs beneath faded turquoise coloured ceiling fans. Why is it that all ceiling fans in China are that same blue-green colour? Half-an-hour before departure, passport control opened, a single booth out of a possible six. Two members of staff were deployed to direct passengers to the correct jetty, bringing the number of staff to a total roughly twice that of the number of passengers. This was as true on board the boat as it was on the shore.

    A terribly sad feeling hung in the air on board and it was also uncomfortably cold even though the outside temperature was twenty-seven degrees Celsius. On this Saturday morning five passengers were leaving for Hong Kong: two foreign business people, a Hongkonger-lookalike who had been talking into his mobile phone since passport control, and two elderly Chinese women. Between them they were unable to fill the boat with any sense of anticipation, with any sense that this was an interesting, exciting journey. In the galley a staff member was filleting a fish but this was not intended for the customers, who instead had to make do with the usual junk food: reconstituted noodles, Pop-Pan biscuits, packets of peanuts or chips, Chinese-manufactured sticky candies and M&Ms. The monotony of the shore line was acute: a maze of industrial buildings punctuated by tall chimneys, docks, container ports, cranes and pylons. All in grey and brown and greige, the colour so beloved of Armani. Greige looks great on the bodies of tall and beautiful women but rather less seductive on the shoreline of an old industrial city.

    Fifteen minutes out, as buildings begin to get lower, the boat picked up some speed but then dropped back to a crawl almost immediately. The local man paused in his telephone conversation to buy a newspaper and a foreigner asked for a can of that universal beverage, Coca-Cola. Half-obscured windows, frosted to soften the sun's glare one assumes, cast an eerie veneer over the shore. It would have been more pleasant to look out through something rose-tinted. A vessel bearing logs and a fishing trawler passed by, but there was very little activity on the water. Greige buildings gave way to red soil and agricultural activity one minute, a tin-roofed fishing village and scrub the next. Now it was old and poor, but the other side of the shore was dotted with plush, three-storey houses finished with white walls and smart grey roofs. All life was inhabiting those shores.

Who is it I know who said whenever he flies to the UK he always takes the Underground from Heathrow to central London because he doesn't want to see all the ugliness of city suburbs from a taxi? Journeying somewhere without seeing where we are going seems to be the preferred way to get around for the well-travelled these days. Boats reveal too much about the landscape and the self. I've read that less than six per cent of travel within the Pearl River Delta is now made by water. Then I was thinking about how construction of roads has lacked synergy with bridges — one of which we were just passing beneath — so that you speed along, only to have to wait endlessly for a car ferry to carry you across a tiny stretch of water. Or wide and impressive bridges which are approached by loosely laid, two-lane roads allowing traffic to move only at a snail's pace. After an hour we docked at some port unknown to me to pick up twenty-five or so passengers. This little excursion added at least thirty minutes to the usual three hour journey and happens rarely, I discovered from a friend later. It does happen if the boat is particularly empty. To count five passengers as empty seems fair enough.

It is no doubt exciting after a few days spent in Guangzhou to see a shiny other civilisation rising out of the water at the end of the journey. One with its own distinct way of being defined by its geographical position, its government, its own people. Even out there on the water a distinctive life and buoyancy could be registered. Boats looked newer and cleaner, they seemed to go faster, and of course there are many more boats in Hong Kong than in any other harbour on the delta. Perhaps watching them was what created the sensation that this Guangzhou–Hong Kong boat was suddenly picking up speed, its inanimate self somehow inspired by the rapid approach of Hong Kong. Something special must blow in the air to make Hong Kong feel the way it does. Off on the shore, a high-rise should have looked like, well, a high-rise. But in Hong Kong even high-rises hold promise and allure, built into hillsides for a range of different heights and configurations. The sky had turned blue and the sun had come out. Buildings looked white, the sea looked blue, the earth looked yellow and the trees looked green. Attributable to the time of day, perhaps, but there was no question that the rest of the journey had been unrelenting in its greyness. Hong Kong splashes on the colour.

Chapter 3: Macau

SUNSET OVER MACAU and across the jagged expanses of the South China Sea was not the rich palate of colours regularly brushed across the beaches of Boracay in the Philippines, or Ko Samui in Thailand. Nor was this sunset framed by palm trees gracefully waving in the early evening breeze. This Pearl River Delta sunset was infused with a light quality specific to southern China waters. Not quite grey and not quite violet, a delicate, pretty light which created gentle contrasts with the peaks rising up from the sea in this island-strewn part of the world, in shades of grey from white-specked to almost black. Even Macau's distinctively yellow-tinged water assumed an attractive, glistening hue. As the sun sets must be the best time to arrive in Macau.

Over the forty-kilometre stretch of water from Hong Kong to Macau which once carried all-night steamers, there now runs the most efficient sea transport system operating in the South China Sea, transporting millions of passengers each year. It is an entirely undemanding journey: you can drink and gamble on board, buy duty-free cigarettes or just eat and read the newspaper. The most regular service, the jetfoil, runs on a powerful Boeing engine and effectively glides on the water — you can't feel this on your own boat but watching the jetfoils going in the opposite direction allows you to see how impressive the boat is.

There are a number of different boats on the Hong Kong to Macau route, including a tired old ferry. A Hong Kong company introduced the Turbo Cat with its exclusive first class service for which you pay a premium — but it is worth it just for the spectacle of the washroom, crafted with an unprecedented flamboyance complete with gold *lamé* toilet seat, mirror framed with a gold-coloured sun and a gold-plated fish-head tap. Passengers on this service get to disembark in an orderly manner before all lower-deck passengers. But the most popular boat is the jetfoil or foilcat, in which Hong Kong businessman Dr Stanley Ho has a considerable interest. It is a splendid complement to the

Macau gambling concession he has held since 1962. Paying passengers get blue tickets; the pink ones are for anyone who has purchased chips in advance. Hotel rooms are often provided free for gamblers, perhaps in one of Dr Ho's own hotels like the gaudy landmark Lisboa. A twenty-four-hour operation which runs four times an hour for most of the day, the jetfoil miraculously maintains an almost clockwork precision, usually making the journey in just under the hour.

It was when the lumbering three-hour ferry journey was cut to a hi-tech one hour that people actually started to visit Macau in any numbers, and what most people visit for is not R&R or conventional tourism — average stay is one-and-a-quarter nights — but for gambling. The relationship between an efficient transport system between Hong Kong and Macau, and the presence of casinos in every major hotel and high-rise building close to the maritime terminal is such that without the one, the other could not survive.

The availability of sea travel from Macau to any other destination besides Hong Kong is scant. Macau's sea link by ferry with Guangzhou was curtailed some months back, there's a single sailing each day to Shenzhen and back, and the only other passenger boat which arrives on the enclave's shores is the tiny little vessel which carries mainlanders and fresh fruit and vegetables throughout the day from Wan Kum on Zhuhai Special Economic Zone's Hengqin Island to Coloane village's toy-town jetty, Ponte Cais de Coloane. A journey of just ten minutes, you need a special day permit to enter Macau this way, and it is very hard for any Macau resident of any nationality to make the return trip. But blind eyes are turned on the produce which makes that trip. Not perishables this time but items like video recorders, television sets and laser disc players are the cargo.

Nor could either the Hong Kong–Macau sea link or the casinos survive if the Chinese were not a race of consummate gamblers. The extent of gambling is such that the tote at one race at the Hong Kong Jockey Club on a Saturday afternoon is equivalent to the combined totes of every race meeting in the United Kingdom on a Saturday afternoon. The Macau Jockey Club has yet to reach such lofty sums, and the dog racing attracts paltry sums by comparison. The casinos,

A Galera, Hotel Lisboa, Macau

on the other hand, account for almost a half of Macau's gross domestic product. In a wealth distribution across the South China Sea, Hong Kong's high spending power has for the past decades breathed life into Macau's otherwise stagnating economy and given the enclave that all-important point of difference without which it would have been lost forever, as good as suffocated by Hong Kong.

Within fifteen minutes from Victoria Harbour the boat was jetting us past the quaint little white-washed houses of the car-free Cheung Chau Island — the Hong Kong to Cheung Chau ferry itself takes almost an hour. Next came the dark, looming peaks of Lantau Island, past the jetty alongside the island's infamous Frog and Toad pub, a failed holiday resort farther along the beach, and a view, on a clear day, of Southeast Asia's largest outdoor bronze Buddha (though he's looking the other way). There was next a section of unbroken water; a bad patch for mobile-phone users when for about ten minutes there was no signal at all. A frustrating but thankfully temporary communication void. Australia may boast the world's highest per capita ownership of mobile phones but Hong Kong is the largest user of them. Before long there was a resurgent chorus of ringing and bleeping as a row of lights appeared on the distant horizon, marking the Macau airport runway stretching out long into the sea. Soon the early evening downtown lights were coming into focus. For a flash it felt like we were discovering another unknown Hong Kong rising inextricably out of the sea, its land masses connected by a pair of bridges. Humble engineering feats compared to Hong Kong's new Tsing Ma suspension bridge, which links the new airport at Lantau Island with the New Territories, Macau's own are nonetheless impressive and lively sights. As the jetfoil swerved sharply to the right and under the newer of the bridges, we were docking at the shiny new terminal under the whipped-up air of the flashy helicopter service which caters to the busy and to the self-indulgent.

Portuguese-administered Macau is an enclave consisting of a peninsula and two islands, a population of 450,000 and a 450-year history which the Portuguese are trying to preserve before it reverts to mainland administration on December 20, 1999. That sense of colonial history is, however, all but being eclipsed by the events of modern history, and most particularly the events of the present decade. Macau is still as pretty as a George Chinnery painting, but beyond colonial Portuguese buildings and tranquil Chinese gardens lurk the ugly realities of a gambling sub-culture.

The casual visitor will likely remain entirely unaware it, but what is going on behind the scenes is fascinating and dangerous. Macau is no longer the stress-free place to which Hong Kong used to turn for a change of pace on the weekend. Paul-Andre Guidat, general manager of the exclusive Bela Vista Hotel, returned to work there in late 1996 for a second stint after a year's absence running a property in Thailand's resort-filled Phuket — and in just one year felt that people in Macau had changed. Not quite as friendly, not quite as open, not quite as relaxed, he said over a glass of Kir in the hotel bar, but he didn't quite know why. Is Macau concerned about 1997, one might ponder? Macau is certainly watching Hong Kong carefully, keen for an indication of what could befall its own administration after 1999.

What has more than anything unsettled the relaxed Macau feeling, and dragged down the mental health of many of its residents, is open warfare, to express it in sensational Hong Kong newspaper terms. The suspected causes of this breach of tranquility and of the presence of these warring factions are several. Imminent return of Hong Kong's sovereignty to the mainland was, according to some sources, pushing the territory's triad activity across the water. But having more impact still, and particularly in the light of the Taiwanese government's crackdown on organised crime, are the daily flights between Macau and Taipei launched when the enclave's international airport was opened in December 1995. The flights do not only carry *bona fide* tourists and businessmen. Another factor is increasing criminal activity emanating from over the border. A robbery on a massive scale at the casino in the Hyatt Regency Taipa in 1994 was thought to have been masterminded by mainlanders — who promptly disappeared back over the border without trace.

Espresso break, Macau

Chapter 3: Macau

By early 1997 it had become clear that not only was every casino operated by triad organisations, but so was each table. Choppings and murders and extortion were becoming almost daily news, and while much of the crime was shrink-wrapped into a one-column story, the murderous attack on a general manager of an international hotel escaped few people's notice. He survived and got back the use of fingers, hands and arms, and believes his golf bag saved his life. Given the intimate dealings with the underground world necessitated by running a hotel with not only a casino but floors allegedly hired out by triads for their private use and that of their clients, a run-in was certainly a feared possibility.

The gambling concession Dr Ho has held for thirty-five years comes up for renewal in 2001. A great deal of lobbying is being undertaken and it remains unclear whether a single franchise will again be granted, or if the concession will be opened out simultaneously to a number of groups. 'China has made it clear that they intend to allow gambling to continue in Macau,' said Dr Ho's nephew, Alan Ho, 'but I don't think they have very much choice. The industrial base is too small; you cannot change the economy that quickly.' Rumours abound that Dr Ho has been talking to the masterminds behind Las Vegas, according to whose vision Macau's gambling infrastructure would likely enlarge still further. While Alan Ho would not comment on those rumours, he doesn't understand why anyone should fear such involvement. What Las Vegas stands for, after all, is family entertainment rather than a dedicated destination for dedicated gamblers. If that resulted in some kind of clean-up in the broader gambling subculture, I can understand Alan Ho's point about the positive effects for Macau of creating a new gambling environment suitable for all kinds of travellers. Pragmatists believe that government efforts to preserve history and develop cultural tourism are fractured and come too late. They believe that properly organised gambling set in a broader context of entertainment for all the family is the only way to a prosperous future for Macau.

The lack of a long-term view on the part of the Macau government should be blamed for this sad demise of a once prosperous outpost, say some, but Macau was never a true colony. Macau has been managed by the Portuguese for 450 years, but nothing more than managed. Nineteen ninety-nine has already happened, some say. In spite of the grandeur which attends the Portuguese administration, Beijing has long been running the city. Every Macau Governor, it is said, is merely a puppet of Beijing. There being no prominent local Chinese to speak of promoted to positions of authority, it's a straight road that leads from the terracotta pink of Government House on the Praia Grande to the unrelenting grey of The Great Hall of the People in Beijing's Tiananmen Square.

Yet when the Portuguese administration offered to hand Macau back to China in a piece of political correctness following the Portuguese Revolution of 1974, China refused and asked the Portuguese to pray continue. Hundreds of years before the Portuguese had successfully cleaned the South China Sea of pirates; the mainland government clearly still believed there were political advantages to having the Portuguese in Macau. The desire to see Taiwan one day willingly and peacefully reunited with the mainland was clearly one of them. Beijing needed time to prepare ways in which Special Administrative Regions could be seen by Taiwan as an attractive reality. The proximity of the British colony of Hong Kong and the demands and assumptions of its succession of governors, against whom Beijing might have felt it needed a little more leverage, was probably another of the advantages of keeping the Portuguese in Macau. Look how smoothly Macau goes, Beijing could say to Hong Kong when Hong Kong fell out of Beijing's preferred line. The pinnacle of the rewards in Macau for all this kowtowing and compliance was an international airport finished long before Hong Kong's. Then, in a visit to Beijing in early 1997 by the president of Portugal, Jorge Sampaio, after a five-day delegation to Macau, came the unlikely acceptance by Jiang Zemin, just days after the death of Deng Xiaoping, of an invitation to visit Portugal.

The Portuguese president's five-day visit to Macau proved to be more than a ceremonial rubber stamping. Lisbon's newspapers in the days following were full of stories about how unhappy he was with certain aspects of the Macau administration and the handover negotiations. The rumours were not confirmed by the Joint Liaison Group, which insisted any ruction had been overplayed, but in March 1997 rifts between the Chinese and Portuguese negotiators erupted for the first time. The rumours suggested finally, after 450 years of peace and compliance, that the Portuguese were making demands on the Chinese. They were on issues like the rights of Macau's indigenous Macanese community; political matters far more sensitive than the proposed conversion of the Bela Vista hotel into the residence of the first Portuguese consul-general to Macau.

On the Chinese side, Lu Ping, director of the Hong Kong and Macau Affairs Office, had publicly cautioned Macau to pay attention to re-establishing law and order and developing its economy ahead of 1999. There are optimists who have been trying to market the enclave as a platform for business, an alternative to Hong Kong which can offer lower rents, a thus-far under-utilised airport little more than ten minutes from downtown, and easy links to the west side of the Pearl River Delta. In this vision of the new Macau, the corporate marketeers may not succeed, so strong is the gambling hook. Few beyond a handful of pioneers who have arrived to set up businesses in Macau have thus far had their perception of the enclave so dramatically altered that they can take it seriously as a business capital. Travelling to the Macau ferry terminal at Hong Kong's Shun Tak Centre (as the majority of the enclave's 8.5 million visitors per year do) via the Mass Transit Railway network, you're hit by myriad posters advertising not the tranquility of the tiny enclave or the developing commercial infrastructure, but the girls you can find in clubs.

The economy may be sluggish and rely heavily on gambling, but Macau is not simply a series of pretty buildings, a saddened and dusty homage to the past completely lacking any contemporary indicators. With its Chinese energy, it is not a place destined to go the way of Malacca which is now little more than a museum documenting Portugal's colonial presence along the straits. Call it ugly, call it spoilt (and plenty do; those who romanticise the place and want Macau to remain pretty and dusty) but the mega-construction work which began in the late 1980s and hasn't let up since is testament to a desire to facilitate the growth and progress of Macau. Macau's land mass has grown from an area of just seventeen square kilometres ten years ago to twenty-one square kilometres. The Macau peninsula consisted of less than three square kilometres in 1840; it now covers nearly seven. Although the population numbers just 450,000, its population density is 21,657 per square kilometre, the highest in the world. Impossibly tiny before, if it was to grow and develop, the enclave needed to find some land, somewhere, and if function overcame form, that was just an unfortunate fact. So while downtown Macau has its old buildings restored, on the outskirts sparkling, if often architecturally horrifying, buildings are steadily going up. This hard, modern edge proves that, against all historic odds, Macau is today an evolving city with its eye on the future.

While businessmen attempt to breathe new life into the enclave to assure it a strong future, architects and academics are attempting to preserve memories of Macau's past. As the most important seafaring nation in Europe, the Portuguese were, in 1557, given the right by officials in Canton to use Macau as a trading base as a complement to their outposts in Goa and Malacca, to facilitate trade between Europe and Asia. Within decades the tiny land mass had become one of the richest places in the world, trading luxuries from around the globe including spices, silk, gems and exotic food products. Macau soon became the accepted place for other European traders to base themselves — British and Dutch-influenced architecture can still be seen, attesting to their long-standing presence and influence. It was during the years following the Opium Wars, after Hong Kong was ceded to the British, that Macau's real decline set in. Macau's history is far longer, but it quickly fell under the long shadow cast by Hong Kong.

Sepia photographs depict tree-lined avenues and 400-year old grand colonial buildings resplendent with columns and arches. The beautifully curving Praia Grande, then the beach road, was the playground of the wealthy, accessed with ease from grand waterfront residences. Gardens full of flowers, homes tended by loyal servants and kitchens full of culinary treats which came in on the ships were the stuff of everyday life for the privileged. Pomp and circumstance attended almost every activity of the Portuguese military. Even the British lived a rose-tinted life, in pre–Hong Kong days headquartering companies and housing families in the enclave in the cause of increasing business with the Chinese. Many aspects of daily life were captured by British artist George Chinnery (1774–1852) whose works appear in public London galleries. Having an artist of his calibre living in Macau served to deliver often poetic images of Macau to a far wider public than images of Hong Kong could ever reach. Chinnery was buried in the enclave's Protestant Cemetery next door to the spectacular former headquarters of the British East India Company and now the enduringly beautiful and peaceful home, complete with weeping willows and fish pond, of the Orient Foundation.

Perhaps those with the most potent stories of Macau life past are the Macanese, the truly indigenous Macau residents, born with Portuguese, Goan, Malaysian, Japanese and Chinese blood running through their veins. Blood from Portugal's Asian colonies, in other words, for when the Portuguese landed in a new country they were encouraged not to plunder but to settle down, marrying into the community and integrating themselves with it.

The Macanese until recently spoke their own patois, combining Cantonese and Portuguese with snatches of other Asian languages like Malay and Tagalog from the Philippines. The Macanese took over the kitchen and produced their own cuisine which, more than a simple cross of Portuguese and Chinese food, crucially combines warm Asian spices like star anise and cinnamon with European herbs such as rosemary. They developed their own unique sub-culture which included eating with spoons and forks rather than chopsticks, and celebrating a British, rather than Portuguese, Christmas complete with plum pudding. Today, accounting for what various estimates place as low as 10,000 out of Macau's total population, the Macanese see themselves defining the enclave less and less with the approach of December 1999. The more established families still run some of

Macau's larger companies; the less established with their facility in English as well as Portuguese and Cantonese have proved invaluable interpreters and middle-men. Some have opened restaurants serving authentic Macanese dishes like *lacassa, chamussas* and *minchi*.

Henrique de Senna Fernandes, whose Portuguese grandmother was born in Shanghai's International Concession, can trace his family back at least 230 years in Macau. Well past retirement age, he still bases himself at his legal practice on Macau's central Avenida Almeida Ribeiro, where he signs a few documents but spends most of his time transcribing his hand-written novels into a computer, editing his own work on the screen. Two of his novels, simple tales written in Portuguese which chart the life of the Macanese in Macau over the last hundred years, have been reworked for the big screen. 'I look in the mirror every day and ask myself: "What surprises will there be today?"' is the way Senna Fernandes described his zest for living and for writing. 'There's always something, however small. Someone who calls, something you see.' He also referred to surprises when he was talking about the return of Hong Kong and Macau to mainland sovereignty. He once worked as a history teacher ('a very good — and immodest — one,' he chuckled) and it is perhaps based on that expertise that he makes the statement: 'History is all surprises.'

So he for one is making no guesses about whether Macau will remain a comfortable place for him to live after 1999. He already has two houses in Portugal, one in Lisbon and one in the country, but why should he want to leave Macau? 'The Macanese *are* Macau,' he said, puffing on a pipe and wrinkling his brow. 'We will resist the Chinese way to do things.' He will go so far as to say that Hong Kong will never be assimilated into the mainland and that it should, rather, with all its brains, motivations and exemplary legal system, be declared a city state like Singapore. 'I told Emily Lau that once right here in my office,' he said, referring to a high-profile Hong Kong Legislative Council member who worked as a journalist before she entered politics. 'But she never printed it.'

There's a decadence about Macanese people like Senna Fernandes which evokes tales of the Burghurs in Ceylon before independence

Henrique de Senna Fernandes, Macau

was announced, of the French in Saigon, or of Shanghainese society in the pre-war and pre-communist 1930s. There's a love of the good life and memories of glorious Sunday lunches for all the family, waited on by a swell of servants. Four- or five-day trips to Hong Kong were very much part of life. Senna Fernandes can still remember the Hong Kong store his mother frequented for buying coffee, owned by a Greek man on Pedder Street. 'The same mix today Mrs Fernandes?' the Greek would ask every time and then prepare the blend 'like a dancer' Senna Fernandes recalled. I'm clearly not the first person to whom Senna Fernandes has recounted this story. These were the days when passports and identity cards were not required to travel between Hong Kong and Macau, when the boat took five hours, and when a full English breakfast at the Cecil Hotel in Central, much beloved by Senna Fernandes, cost HK$1.20.

Remnants of the lifestyles of the Macanese and Portuguese ruling class in days gone by remain, and not only in the memories of the oldest members of the best Macanese families, or in lavish, Portuguese-administered museums chronicling the enclave's extraordinary rises and falls, and the introduction to Asia of Portuguese culture, everything from wine to the *lorcha,* a Portuguese pirate-catching vessel. 'You feel Portuguese every day,' concurred lawyer and sympathetic long-term Macau resident Francisco Gonçalves Pereira, from his office-with-a-view in the Luso Building. He chooses to live downtown with what he calls its 'Mediterranean' features rather than in a more obvious expatriate residential ghetto. 'The Portuguese community has many familiar things here. The Leal Senado, the coffee, the bookstore.... It is an atmosphere which has been reinforced during the last decade'.

Such reinforcement as Gonçalves Pereira perceives it has much to do with a rash of last-minute rebuilding and restoration projects sanctioned by a government in some degree of panic. Restoration work funded by the current administration and effected by Portugal's leading landscape architect, Francisco Manuel Caldeira Cabral, for example, has returned Largo do Senado, the area in front of the Leal

Senado (the seat of government), to an attractive paved area. Using traditional Portuguese *calçada,* (small paving stones) laid out in formations to suggest waves, and featuring a globe in the middle of a fountain to symbolise the seafaring traditions of the Portuguese, it at once creates a sense of history while providing a solution to a contemporary problem, and that is lack of open space for residents. Complete with renovated and freshly painted facades overlooking the square, here, right in the centre of town, all can enjoy a leisurely stroll or just sit and watch the multi-faceted world wander by.

Similarly impressive projects undertaken by Portuguese architect and Macau resident Bruno Suares, who works in partnership with his wife, Irene, have included the renovation of the historic, British-designed Bela Vista Hotel with its columned outdoor terrace into an exclusive eight-suite affair. The terracotta pink-and-white-painted Clube Militar at the city end of the Praia Grande has been restored to its former atmosphere and glory, complete with original mirrors and chandeliers and stunning night-time exterior lighting. The club's colonial dining room, open to the public with a well-conceived Portuguese menu and wine list, is the most handsome dining room in Macau. Suares has made a positive spectacle out of buildings like the magnificent yellow-painted Autoridade Monetaria on Rua de Pedro Nolasco da Silva, destined to become the Portuguese Consulate after 1999.

All those involved in such work feel that restoration of some of the enclave's most impressive buildings is less colonial excess and more a case of being true to history. Nor is attention only being paid to the Portuguese-ness of Macau. Cabral, with an informed sensitivity to both occidental and oriental traditions, is responsible for the acclaimed garden of Canal dos Patos, close to the border, feted as a marvellously successful example of how the two traditions can be married. Cabral has also worked on the area surrounding A-Ma Temple, a structure which marks the birth of Macau long before the Portuguese arrived. Too many historic buildings have their impact ruined by development around them, and it is this problem which Cabral is addressing at this temple. First he moved out the buses, and then he cobbled the road to ensure that cars slow down as they drive past.

In moves which might upset the purist, new downtown Macau buildings seek to echo the European architecture around them and, even worse to some minds, other developments are going up behind facades of original buildings. Such activity is hardly surprising in a city forced by history to redefine itself and its position in Asia if it wishes to survive. While it may be the case that Soares does not approve of these practices from an architectural point of view, he believes that given Macau's space pressure, it is a compromise that can be lived with. The alternative is to lose everything from the architectural and cultural past, and subsequently all attendant memories and imaginings.

The Instituto Cultural Macau (ICM), a non-profit organisation founded in 1982 with a remit to preserve Macau's cultural heritage, is by definition convinced that Macau is a culturally rich city worthy of preservation, though it also looks to the future. The institute has taken a key role in the formation of the Fundacio Sino-Latin de Macau in an attempt to give Macau a new and important role in the period after handover. 'If our Sino-Latin culture is lost, we will become another small city in China, and even worse than other small cities because we are that much smaller,' said Gary Ngai, a gently spoken Indonesian-born Chinese who has lived in Macau for twenty years and works as one of ICM's three vice-presidents. 'It is in the interests of China to preserve Macau's culture because China needs to connect with the Latin world more and more. In the future Macau could be the crossing point.' The model to his mind is the São Paulo College, built 400 years ago by the Jesuits as the first Western-style college in the Far East, which taught Chinese and Portuguese language and culture, translated books from one language to the other and so on. 'The building may have burned down,' said Ngai, adding rather poetically: 'but the spirit is still here.' The institute believes, in this connection, that the Portuguese language, currently spoken by three per cent of Macau's population though Ngai said experts believe others simply choose not to speak it in favour of Cantonese or English, should and will be increasingly taught and adopted after 1999. Just as the Macanese, with their embrace of Western and Eastern

Ruins of St Paul's Church, Macau

Chapter 3: Macau

languages and cultures, have allowed the Portuguese and Chinese to communicate with each other in Macau, Ngai and the new foundation's board believe that Macau itself can fulfil such a role but this time on a global scale between China and the Latin world.

Such activity surely comes too late and the ideas sound fanciful. Colonial sentimentality attends any discussions about Macau as a model of a centuries-long peaceful coexistence of East and West. The relationship between the Portuguese and the Chinese is at best one characterised by passive acceptance. The Chinese eat lunch in Chinese restaurants at noon; the Portuguese eat lunch in Portuguese restaurants at 1:30PM, and that observation just highlights the most overt indicators of the separation of cultures within the enclave.

Even in Macau's earliest days, Portuguese traders may have married local or Asian women and employed local or Asian women in their homes, but the power balance was always uneven and remains so. There has been no localisation policy even during the final decade of foreign administration: the Chinese in Macau still lack the education, financial resources and overall sophistication of their Hong Kong compatriots. The Macanese represent the most literal coming together of two cultures, but they spawned their own sub-culture and while serving as a bridge between Chinese and Portuguese, have not brought the two cultures closer together in any deep sense. There is little understanding by the Chinese of the Portuguese and vice versa, the lack of any shared language playing a major part in this inability to appropriate each other's cultures. One respected Portuguese academic pointed out that the Macanese are being subsumed by Chinese culture because the women are now forced to marry Chinese men, when in the past there were a greater number of eligible Portuguese men, such as the military, living in the enclave.

Portuguese visiting Macau from Portugal are for their part left disappointed by the enclave. Initially impressed by the smart new buildings alongside old Portuguese architecture, the evocative Portuguese street names and the Portuguese wine and olive oil on the shelves of every corner store, they are led to expect far more Portuguese day-to-day culture than they can subsequently find. The number of Portuguese residents has dwindled to little over 3,000, and very few people beyond that community speak Portuguese. The Portuguese expatriate community itself is, with the odd exception, an insular and homogeneous group. Almost all occupy official and civil service rather than business positions and many arrive fresh from other backwater Portuguese colonies; they are a different breed to the corporate-heavy expatriate communities of cities like Hong Kong, Singapore and Tokyo — and the inability to speak English is unfortunately a deficiency in Asia. In these larger cities, expatriates tend to appropriate the speed and efficiency of business dealings in Asia into their own professional lives, and develop a fascination for the way their own sense of self integrates with their new surroundings. Leaving Asia's most exciting cities to return to their home countries then becomes increasingly untenable. But this stimulating mood passes by the Portuguese community in contemporary Macau who are interested in saving money and then leaving. That is the majority, anyway; people in jobs they're either ill-equipped to handle or simply disinterested in, but who possess the right kind of military background and thus access to the right network to put them in those jobs.

In contrast, the casual observer of, rather than participant in Portuguese culture, and particularly the observer who lives in Asia and not the West, finds Macau alluringly European in mood and style. No doubt the marked Portugueseness of the Portuguese expatriate community contributes heavily to this impression. The golden days are still upon the enclave, or so it looks. The Portuguese have their own television channel, their own newspapers, their own radio station and their own bookshop. Top Portuguese wines brought in with barely a tax slapped on them can be readily purchased at the supermarket, bread and coffee are second to none in Asia, and charm-infused Portuguese restaurants serving authentic dishes allow Portuguese expatriates to eat their own food from menus in their own language — with often barely another tongue to be heard in the place. Unbelievably, when you compare the enclave to Hong Kong and the high ranks held by the territory's Chinese, almost all senior jobs in Macau are still held by heavily bearded Portuguese men who are chauffeured around in black limousines — well, at least old black cars — driven by smooth skinned Chinese wearing white gloves. What non-Portuguese visitors also tune into is the Latin *mañana*, the almost languid feel to proceedings, whether those proceedings are diplomatic rituals, business meetings, or a coffee before work at Bolo de Arroz. You'd be forgiven for thinking the entire Portuguese community floods through this café's doors. Modern and stylish, it is a positive showcase for almost every kind of Portuguese pastry and is one of the best places for an espresso in the whole of Asia, drunk Iberian style, of course, standing up at the counter. In that swell of Portuguese language and Portuguese cigarette smoke, it proves hard for even the non-smoker to resist the temptation to light up.

The infectious appeal of Coloane Island similarly owes everything to the enclave's lazy colonialism. Twenty minutes in a taxi from downtown brought me to the island as the setting sun was casting deep shadows through the weaving trunks and broad-set branches of the beautiful old banyan trees and onto the village's cobbled streets. All was still and besides the odd motorbike or the chug chug of a tiny fishing boat out towards the nearest mainland China post of Wan Kum, all that could be heard was the chitchat of contented little birds, the persistent shuffles of tiles on the mahjong table, and the laughter of children playing some variation on soccer on the square. Oh, and the sound of Warren Rooke, well-known Hong Kong media figure, hammering together wooden crates for his wife, Anita Lauder, who runs an antiques business from the village's narrow streets and needed to get a shipment packed before dusk — but was personally down with shingles. Anita and Warren bought a house in the village in the late 1970s as a weekend bolt-hole from pressured lives in Hong Kong — but have now almost entirely exchanged the stresses of high-rise Hong Kong for village life and a full-on business. A kite soared powerfully overhead and the smell of wok-fried vegetables rose from a traditional little house down by the waterfront.

Coloane, with just 2,500 inhabitants, is one of Southern China's most tranquil spots, a favoured retreat of Hongkongers who go there to play golf, relax on a private balcony at the vast Westin Resort hotel, take the longest lunch of clams in white wine and chili prawns at the popular beachside Fernando's restaurant, or drink a bottle of *vinho verde* on the terrace of the rather more idiosyncratic Pousada de Coloane hotel. Until as recently as the beginning of the century the island was inhabited almost exclusively by mainland Chinese pirates along with São Francis Xavier, who gave his name to the village's tiny chapel, with its single bell rung on Sunday mornings, as well as a bone from one of his arms. (The remainder of his anatomy is buried on Shangchuan Island, a tourist attraction complete with casinos west of Macau in the South China Sea).

Rush Coloane and you miss the point; a place where the bank and the post office attract fewer customers each day than there are staff to run them. It does not work to get out of a taxi in Coloane's village square and make straight for an exquisite dinner of *casquinhas* (baked crab) and *arroz de cabidela* (duck rice) at Portuguese-owned Cacarola restaurant, however good you've heard the restaurant is. And it is good, probably Macau's most consistent and authentic Portuguese restaurant. You can't rush straight in for dinner because you have to give the island the honour of a few minutes of your focus; you have to take time to walk around and feel its charms. It is hard to tell which is public right-of-way and which is someone's living space. You virtually have to step over tables and chairs or washing machines and washing lines to make your way about the village. Up and down the village's little *travessa*s and *rua*s mostly impassable by cars, so perfectly are the crumbling walls and peeling facades of Chinese and Portuguese architecture melded after all these years that it is hard to tell where one starts and the other finishes; like the face of an old man imparted with character and experience rather than colour or ethnicity.

There is nothing like returning from Macau into Hong Kong's dizzyingly busy and ever-shrinking harbour — environmentalists worry that the famous Victoria Harbour which made Hong Kong a great port will become little more than Victoria River — to realise how peaceful Macau manages in so many ways to be. Stress levels in cities are determined by factors such as how fast elevator doors close, but could also be measured by the angles and stability, or otherwise, of gangplanks. Stepping off the boat is the first of many stressful experiences laid on by Hong Kong, so high and rough have the waves become in the face of massive land reclamation. Pushing and shoving are one thing in this part of the world, but most of the passengers simply cannot help but bounce off each other as they try to get off the vessel safely, clutching a piece of Louis Vuitton luggage under one arm and a child under the other. Hong Kong perceives open warfare on the streets of Macau. To Macau, Hong Kong has another kind of warfare out there on its streets, one which has nothing to do with the triads and everything to do with getting swept up in one of the fastest-moving cities in the world.

Chapter 4: The west side

ZHUHAI IS LITERALLY A STONE'S THROW from Macau if you're strong on the upper-arm; a five-minute walk from the civilised setting of Macau's smart terminal building adorned with Portuguese tiles at Portas do Cerco through scrubland to the battered old terminal building and uneven pavements of Gongbei, the southernmost point of the Zhuhai Special Economic Zone (SEZ). The border was created some 400 years ago, traversed daily by the Chinese who serviced the Portuguese in Macau but were not allowed to live there.

As recently as fifteen years ago Zhuhai, or more specifically Gongbei, was not popularly considered a stone's throw from Macau but as a rather more challenging two-hour illegal swim. The main street leading to the border today is a thoroughfare which used to run directly along the seafront and as such was able to open only during day-light hours, whether for traffic or pedestrians. There was a very specific reason for restricted access: the street was a favoured access point for the swim which countless Chinese attempted in a quest to reach Macau and, from there, should they wish to go farther, a favoured Western city.

Today, if you know the right person, unlimited travel to Macau from Zhuhai through official channels is hardly exceptional (just produce the necessary money) and plenty of Macau residents would probably prefer to live along one of Zhuhai's wide boulevards than in the crowded enclave. This freedom of movement from Zhuhai similarly applies to residents of Zhongshan, a city one hour north of Zhuhai, who even ten years ago were unable to travel freely as far as Zhuhai for fear they too might take to the waters in their bathers for rather more than a dip.

Around a fifth of Macau's annual visitors now enter the enclave on foot via Gongbei, and many Macau residents pop over the border for a few hours at a time for buying certain items which are far cheaper than in Macau, or to bring for families and friends certain items which are unavailable for purchase in Zhuhai. To find out what those items are it is only necessary to watch what's on the trolleys and in the cartons or bags of those crossing the border. I noticed feather dusters and chocolate cakes in a bag carried by an old chap one morning from Macau, but those tastes are comparatively esoteric. Toilet rolls from Zhuhai are an extremely popular item. Customs officers don't even blink an eyelid at a trolley bearing a dozen packs of a dozen rolls, bound for resale in a store rather than for personal use; the quantity would certainly suggest domestic overkill. Bags and sometimes sacks of fruit and vegetables make the journey back to Macau, though meat is not allowed through.

If Shenzhen is a busy, bustling city in the Hong Kong style, even as it feels like Hong Kong's country cousin, so the atmosphere of Zhuhai reflects its proximity to Macau. More like a town than a city, it is in comparison to Shenzhen calm and collected, and takes quality of life seriously. It boasts wide and well-lit avenues, clean streets and tidy buildings, trees and flowers at every turn, a well-planned road system and a lack of human or vehicular congestion; all these are immediately obvious to national and international visitors alike.

In the west part of the zone, in the direction of Doumen, scrupulous urban planning and vision for the future are even more apparent. An area formerly separated from Zhuhai City by rivers and estuaries, driving there would take half a day, what with waiting around for old-fashioned car ferries and tug boats; the two areas of the SEZ are now connected by a series of extremely impressive, often eight-lane bridges. Hand-laid roads finished to an extremely high standard beam off in every direction, alongside which works are under way at every stage from the flattening of mountains and pulling up of banana plantations to putting the final lick of paint on factories for companies as prestigious as Mercedes-Benz and Canon. All the land in this area was formerly entirely given over to banana plantations. If you're lucky enough to spot such a plantation in this area, 'you better look twice,' I was told by a Eugenio Gili, a Chilean businessman from Hong Kong who is half of a joint venture in Doumen in a factory making in-flight accessories, 'because it will be

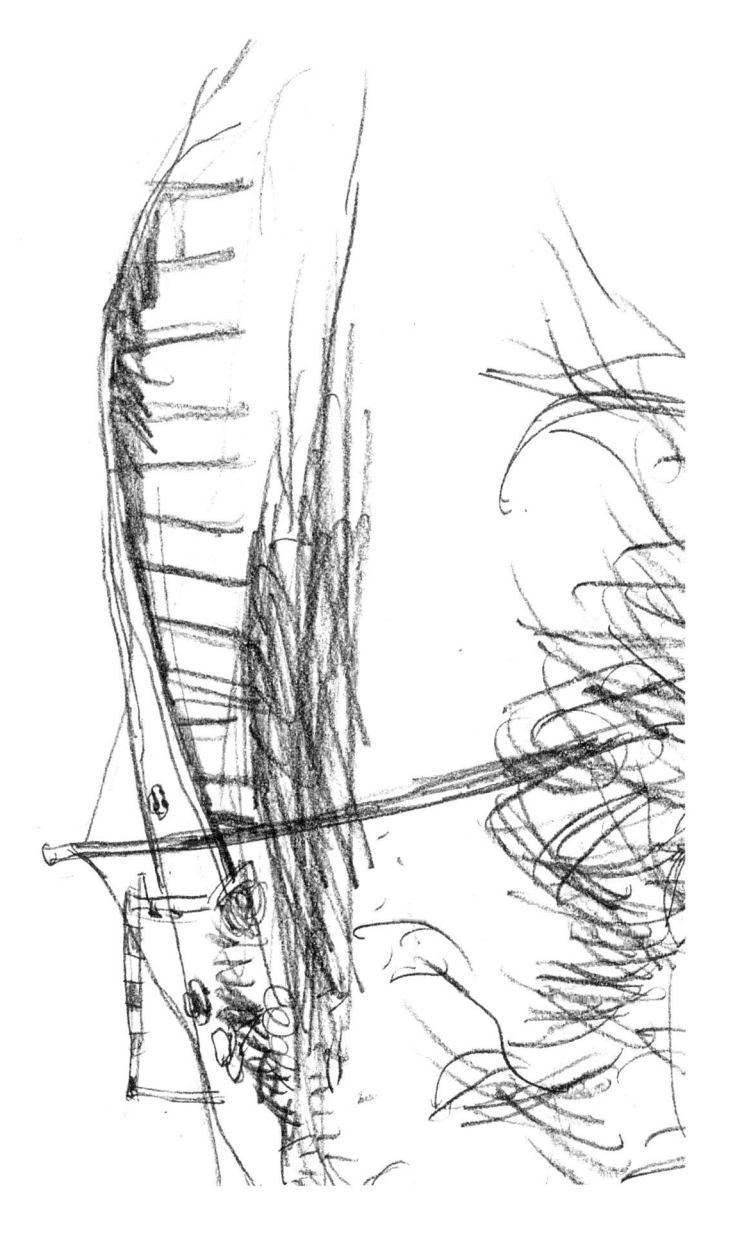

Bridge, Zhuhai

gone next time you drive down this road.' Mr Gili has been doing business in the area for fifteen years and if he leaves more than a few months between visits, he barely recognises the place on his return.

DEVELOPMENT IS THE ONLY WAY declares a huge banner on the way to the airport; LET THE WORLD KNOW ZHUHAI, LET ZHUHAI COME TO THE WORLD reads another. According to the original plan, Macau was to have an international airport, while Zhuhai's airport would operate on a national level. Once the new highway connecting Macau with the mainland is in place, they will be little more than thirty minutes apart. The synergy sounds promising, although flights to various cities in China, almost always filled with Taiwanese who still cannot fly direct to the mainland, is an all-important feature of the Macau operation. One visit to Zhuhai airport, however, itself already something of a weekend tourist attraction, and it is clear that the Mayor of Zhuhai has other ideas about the role of his airport and its importance in the overall development of the zone. Right now it operates flights to as many as thirty domestic destinations each day and is suffering huge losses, but there is no question that it looks like an international rather than a domestic airport. Announcements are made in English as well as Mandarin. It has almost as many gates as there are destinations in China. Apparently the most hi-tech airport in China, it is surely the best-designed too. The restaurant, clean and conceived to appeal to international travellers, serves cookies with its coffee and in a country heavily targeted by cigarette companies as a growth market, does not provide ashtrays unless such are requested.

Zhuhai may lag behind Shenzhen in industrial output, and lack a deep-sea port (there will be one close to the airport in the future), but in following in at least some of Shenzhen's footsteps this zone has been able to watch the development of its sister zone very carefully, and thus avoid many of the urban development problems suffered by Shenzhen. Zhuhai is planning for the future — anticipating, for example, a direct bridge link within a few years. The dedicated new expressway leading straight to Macau is already under construction. On what were vast stretches of lush agricultural land around the airport, the Zhuhai government has planned attractive avenues of houses, often nestling on hillsides with full sea views, has put in facilities like wet markets, flattened sites ready for industrial buildings and has, of course, laid down wide roads which are supremely under-utilised today. The sums of money invested in this, an infrastructure for the future, is beyond imagination.

Zhuhai is clearly placing as much emphasis on developing tourism as on attracting foreign businesses, and certainly it has far more appeal than other parts of Guangdong Province, with the notable exceptions of the mountains and lakes of Zhaoqing to the west of Guangzhou. Zhuhai doesn't have the gambling facilities, essential to Macau's tourism appeal, but it does have a Formula One race track (Macau only attracts Formula Three) and hosts one of China's three film festivals. But with beach-side hotels, holiday houses and bungalows, it is relying more on assets like natural beauty and clean air for holidays with an appeal for all the family. Imagining the day when Chinese from north of the zone will own holiday homes here, flying in for the weekend to be whisked off for a spot of golf, a seafood dinner and a walk on the beach, comes easy.

Even the area just outside downtown Zhuhai, really the heart of the zone, has the sea to one side and a stretch of forested mountains to the other, and looks much more attractive than even the prettiest parts of Hong Kong's New Territories. The water quality is high when compared to Hong Kong, and vast fishing nets, suspended at four corners, run the length of the ocean road. The main industrial zone, planned so that each factory or company is responsible for one block, is situated twenty minutes from the main city, and even this is comparatively clean. Some of the factories are more like something from a new town's strictly controlled industrial park in the United Kingdom. Even here there is something of a seaside resort feel (although there is only one small beach for swimming) with a wide coast road, huge fun park called Pearl Land with rollercoaster, big wheel, children's entertainment, and nearby luxury golf course.

The bulk of tourists are from neighbouring Zhongshan County rather than people arriving via Hong Kong or Macau, and they are already flocking to the New Yuan Ming Palace, Zhuhai's answer to

Chapter 4: The west side

Shenzhen's Splendid China. A walk up the 'Great Wall' offers expansive views as far as Macau, though however well the theme park has been effected, cleverly landscaped into hills which create the perfect backdrop for the brightly coloured temples, it is ultimately kitsch and bears no relation to the feel of the original Yuan Ming Yuan (Summer Palace) in Beijing. But it caters to a demand, as does Zhuhai's new, prized hotel, the five-star Grand Bay View. The property commands room rates equivalent to those in Macau but is famed not as a tourist destination in its own right but as a 'safe house' for regional businessmen who wish to entertain, or to be entertained by local women. Said to be owned by a prominent member of the Guangzhou police force, the local officials have scant power in such a presence. Should a Hong Kong or Macau businessman be caught at one of Zhuhai's notorious 'hair salons', he had better have a minimum of HK$5,000 in his jacket pocket, or he risks being detained on the mainland for a questionable time by the get-tough police department. At this hotel, cash or no cash, he can come and go as and when he pleases.

Pronounced a Special Economic Zone in the early 1980s, shortly after Shenzhen had become the first SEZ, the changes to Zhuhai since that time have been remarkable, even more so considering that fertile agricultural land then dominated the region. Back in the pre-reform days it was little more than a fishing village and agricultural community, and its inhabitants, even if they didn't know each other's names, would recognise each other on the street. Today, less than an estimated ten per cent of the population are Zhuhai-born. Drive for just ten minutes and you probably pass through six or seven different villages with their own names, now subsumed in the conglomeration.

What has happened for its residents in less than a generation is extraordinary. In a kitchen luxuriously large by Hong Kong standards there's a sink with running water — but next to it evidence of an old well, now inoperative but as few as fifteen years ago the only source of fresh water. Not every home had its own well — some people needed to walk considerable distances to obtain fresh water — with the result that water 'theft' was not unknown. Pao Lin-kan, born in

Chapter 4: The west side

Zhuhai but a resident of Macau for the past fifteen years, remembers lowering the water melons into that well to cool the fruit during the hot summer months. The low-temperature-enhanced taste was delicious. Pao, chief engineer for an international hotel in Macau, married a woman from Zhongshan in his early twenties at a time when they were both employed at another hotel in Macau, and with her is bringing up in Macau two sons, aged seven and nine. 'They're always fighting!' he said.

I went to Zhuhai one day with Pao, who doesn't have an English name but has thought about adopting one and is very happy to be called Lincoln. I joined him on a visit to his parents in the large, two-storey but very simple white-brick house where he was brought up with his two elder sisters. The only real differences to the house since the days when Lincoln lived there are the huge dog kept for security purposes in the front yard and the three-storey residential building in the back yard. Lincoln and the younger of his sisters, who also lives in Macau, financed the building of this small apartment block, the rental of which supports their parents. It is a nice take on the Chinese tradition of supporting other members of the family. This way, said Lincoln, his parents can take personal responsibility for their income, and should he suddenly wish to throw in his job or start his own business, he would have no worries about lacking the financial resources to continue to support his parents.

The parents live a simple life in a no-frills environment, the highlight of which is the visit of one of their children or grandchildren. Still in good health, they both take a walk or some exercise in the morning, chat to the neighbours, visit the nearby market to buy food each day, and in the evening watch television. By day the set, shelved alongside various figures and symbols of Chinese culture, is covered with a coloured cloth, as though its presence is not quite right. Neither can read or write. Lincoln's father is the solid, silent type, but his mother, as well as having a beautiful smile, is a marvellous and animated conversationalist, a rare skill she's passed on to her son. She was delighted that I enjoyed the Chinese tea she poured for me and took me off to the kitchen to show me the well which Lincoln had previously mentioned. It was tough work getting water from the well and this she told me not in Cantonese but in a show of how her muscles would ache after the drawing of a single bucket. The parents just worry about their youngest daughter who, in her mid-thirties, remains unmarried. Can their son not introduce her to a good man, they constantly ask? Lincoln thinks his sister has been scared off marriage by the large number of divorces — and second divorces — she's seen within her circle of friends. But it is a difficult concept to explain to elderly parents on the mainland.

When I asked Lincoln's parents if they preferred Zhuhai today or before it became a Special Economic Zone, they didn't appear to understand the question. This is their home; that seemed to be the message. They are clearly part of the older generation which has watched, with varying degrees of often unconscious bewilderment, as their small, friendly village has been transformed into an internationally-known SEZ. A hillside close to their home was designated suitable for building. Construction work had already begun on a series of government buildings when the area was declared by a *fung shui* expert to be a terrible mistake. The site was levelled, the trees were replanted, and the construction company moved on. Still, if a *fung shui* expert could influence the angle of the escalators leading up to the public banking floors of Sir Norman Foster's landmark Hongkong & Shanghai Bank headquarters in Hong Kong's Queen's Road Central, the aborted construction and resultant patch of young green trees on a hillside in Zhuhai should come as no surprise.

Mr Ng lived close to Lincoln's family as a child, attended the same school as Lincoln, and remains one of his best friends. Unlike many of their classmates, one of whom Lincoln hears runs his own trading company in Hong Kong and is 'a very rich man', Mr Ng has never left Zhuhai, though he's hoping to visit Macau within the next few months. He is a perfect illustration of what his generation has had the opportunity to achieve even within the confines of Zhuhai City.

Tall, attractive according to a more northern-Chinese aesthetic, and quietly spoken, Mr Ng drives a beige-coloured Lexus with

Chapter 4: The west side

matching interior. I commented favourably on the car but was immediately told it was only a 300. 'Everyone's talking about the 400 now'. Although the number plate begins with the letter 'C', suggesting it is a Zhuhai company-owned car, (privately owned car number plates begin with 'A'), there was something to suggest that he may have had the opportunity to buy it. There are stories of long-term employees being allowed to buy their company-owned residential accommodation at as low as RMB30,000 for a 1,000 square metre apartment. Multiply that by ten for the commercial rate. So perhaps Mr Ng was offered some similar kind of deal on the car. Certainly his business successes, although modest in comparison with 'big' businessmen in Zhuhai, are still considerable and, more importantly, confirm the importance of connections. 'Good business' in China, suggested Lincoln when I asked him about the most lucrative jobs in Zhuhai, has less to do with the products or services offered or even the ability to predict trends and get there first, and more to do with good relationships with other businesses. Crucially, he added, success in business has to do with good relationships with people in administrative authority. In Mandarin the word for such connections is *guanxi* — and it is fittingly one of the best-known Chinese words in the Western world.

Mr Ng runs a pair of back-to-back restaurants in a building owned by the Bank of China. He is related by marriage to the former head of the bank's branch in Zhuhai, and was given the opportunity to take over a restaurant which was losing money. Halving the size of the kitchen, he created two restaurants in one — a fast-food shop in the front and an *à la carte* restaurant behind it, complete with private rooms ideal for business people who do not wish to have their conversations overheard. He put in fish tanks and poultry crates and personally goes to market each morning to buy produce. He spends the best part of the day — and night — at the restaurant and should he leave the premises, his mobile phone rings constantly. As he drove, a call came in from a customer who was planning to dine at the restaurant that night, requesting turtle soup. Mr Ng immediately turned the car around and headed for Zhuhai's marvellous fish market

— the variety is far greater than in Macau, Lincoln observed — and picked out a turtle which he carried back to the car in a blue plastic bag, its head popping out at the top from time to time. He dropped the creature off with the chef. It's all about keeping customers happy, several of whom probably make up Mr Ng's *guanxi* network.

The restaurant has a black ceiling decorated with faux foliage, agricultural paraphernalia on the walls and wooden tables and chairs. These were oiled and flamed before being sanded down and varnished to create the illusion of traditional old furniture. Over clams in black bean sauce, steamed fish and braised vegetables, we chatted about the economics of it all. Food costs amount to around RMB100,000 month, fixed costs to about RMB30,000, staff costs to about RMB40,000. Mr Ng reckons he takes about RMB300,000 per month. Lincoln quickly estimated that Mr Ng makes RMB100,000 per month from this food operation. Mr Ng has a second restaurant up and running, another about to open and, more important still, has just paid RMB4 million for a two-storey downtown property the size of a McDonald's. The most interesting thing is that Mr Ng has a full-time job quite apart from his burgeoning restaurant business, but thanks to another bit of *guanxi* he is not required to turn up at the office more than once or twice a week. There is no one there who would dare criticise.

Lincoln is not, and has never been, particularly happy in Macau. For him, an airy apartment — actually, make that a house — with a sea view to the front and trees to the back is his ultimate residence. This he could have in Zhuhai but he doesn't much want to return there — 'unless I was a rich man,' he said. He has a very good idea of how much people earn. Those at the Gongbei border crossing who sit in front of a little desk with a couple of telephones on it charge one yuan for a local call and about RMB10 for a three-minute call to Hong Kong or Macau. Not the way to make millions, but underneath the desk is a calculator and a stack of notes, for they are also money changers. Telephones and money changing can generate up to RMB5,000 a month. Girls working in the notorious hair salons, or rather invariably sitting outside them and offering something rather more exotic than a short back and sides, can earn up to RMB20,000 a month. The innocent traveller who genuinely wants a haircut gets quite a surprise.

For all the wealth which drives up and down the highways in the form of a beige-coloured Lexus 300 or yellow Porsche, or participates in extravagant ordering in the type of restaurants which take pride in their white linen, only one in 100 Zhuhai SEZ residents has crossed any kind of material threshold. Between the three-lane highways, should you take a left or a right turn, are tiny lanes barely wide enough for a car along which a man may be having his hair cut as he looks into a mirror suspended from a tree, or someone may be selling half-rate fruit they've scavenged from the market. Roads lined with hi-fi shops and pharmacies might also have a row of shoe repairers sitting on their haunches on the pavements outside. Bicycles, once an endearing symbol of China's unique lifestyle, abound along these lanes. But here they're no more than a symbol of the poverty which endures even in a go-getting city-county like Zhuhai. Most residents still earn around RMB1,000 per month, down to as little as RMB500 or RMB600 for a waitress and RMB300 for a factory worker, their struggle all the greater in the face of the opulence around them.

The constant movement of humanity and their plastic bags between Zhuhai and Macau apart, Zhuhai's proximity to Macau makes little different to the SEZ's economic well-being or indeed its culture. That minutes away is a spot of old China administered for centuries by a Western power is of no consequence to this vision of the new China. But travel north to Zhongshan City — on a road far safer than that running north from Shenzhen — and the extent of the influence and historical activity of the Portuguese along the Pearl River Delta is there to be seen.

In what is often regarded as a tragic cost of progress, the original centre of a city today undergoing development is usually of no relevance to the new thrust, often resulting in its entire destruction. Such destruction is rarely a loss for those living in the cities. As Singapore's Lee Kuan Yew has insightfully suggested, it is usually the Western tourist who wants to see pretty buildings — just before retreating to the hi-tech comforts of a modern five-star hotel. But Zhongshan is one city which lives comfortably with both past and future even along a single street.

A third of the population of Macau was originally from Zhongshan City, an agriculturally rich area like so much of the west side of the Pearl River Delta. The city has seen enormous building and modernisation programmes in the last fifteen years, and has won the award for China's cleanest city. In March 1997, the city became the first in China to outlaw the car horn. The four-star Zhuhai International Hotel opened about ten years ago, and it remains the focal and meeting point of the city's emerging business community. All pillars and marbles and shiny floors, one member of staff of this property seemed to be employed purely to keep the floor spotless. A blue Jaguar pulled up outside, a pair of local businessmen stepped out and walked into the lobby; the woman and her broom where soon there to rapidly wipe away any trace of dusty footprints. The lobby lounge, minimum order RMB10, was buzzing with conversation and the sound of mobile phones. Three foreign businessmen clambered out of the back of a van and walked awkwardly across to the reception desk. 'They're new to China,' observed my Hong Kong friend, Lau Kin-wai: 'They're not expatriates from Hong Kong.' I know it is not difficult for the practiced eye to visually differentiate between Chinese from Hong Kong, Taiwan and the mainland, but this was the first time I'd heard anyone register and expound the difference between a foreign businessman living in Asia and one visiting from his home country. Oh, the power of non-verbal and quite unintentional communication.

Zhongshan is not an easy city to visit if you're a foreign businessman with little China consciousness. But it does have a McDonald's and there's something reassuring about finding a McDonald's in a city, even if you don't eat beef and hold mass American culture in low regard. This branch is across the city's famous bridge which splits into two as it rises to facilitate the passing of large ships, though no ships of that stature use this waterway now. As in most cities in the world, McDonald's has an excellent location which wraps the restaurant around two corners of a busy junction. Floor-to-ceiling glass walls are spotlessly clean and reveal a thriving business inside.

But look up to the first floor, and then at the entire first floor of this narrow, main street with stores spilling out onto the bustling pavements, and you see a stretch of European architecture. Dutch-style warehouses and Portuguese-style houses painted in yellow and green are immediately evocative of Macau, complete with shutters and balconies and delightful little decorative details. In this city, adding to its downtown charm, cycle-rickshaws are actually hailed by local residents; they're far more than the tourist attraction they've become in Macau where really it is too polluted to sit on one for long. The human-proportioned Coca-Cola and Fanta bottles which sit by the roadside in Macau's Taipa and Coloane islands are a bizarre Macau icon, the result of a marketing campaign from decades back before Diet Coke was even thought of. And there, on a road just out Zhongshan, is an identical bottle. Sometimes the Pearl River Delta feels like a tiny village.

Because Zhongshan has not pulled down its traditional downtown to make way for high-rises, Lau Kin-wai can even point out the old house where he was born and lived until the age of seven, above a new stationery and accessories shop selling everything from calligraphy pens to colourful lion heads and drum kits. Unprotected wads of electrical wires traverse the street as they did when he was a lad, now as then a favourite landing place for swallows. Kin-wai was obviously enjoying the visit to his old home town, commenting on the intimacy and leisurely feel of the old quarter. He took me down one alley to a little shop where an old man was tirelessly ladling ink and hand-printing business cards. Kin-wai put in an order, complete with a full-colour painting on the flip-side, arranging to have the cards sent on to him in Hong Kong. 'New York feels more like home than here,' he said, walking through the vegetable market busy with shoppers on their way home from work to cook dinner. 'The culture, the people, the jazz; it is easy to communicate in New York . . . these are the things I like.'

Printer, Zhongshan

Chapter 4: The west side

Kin-wai can entirely relate to the local food, though, and it was off with his cousin to dinner in Gangkou, some fifteen minutes away by car — and you need a car to get there unless you are prepared to invite your taxi driver to join your party as a way of ensuring that he stays put to take you back to the city. The restaurant is in the middle of nowhere, accessed along a rather rough but pretty road at the side of the river. White ducks are secured in wire cages at the water's edge by the fishing huts, and there are many boats out on the water. The restaurant is similarly attractive, built of bamboo, and clean inside if you don't include the toilets and the vast, open kitchen in the equation. But the tables and chairs are clean, as are the fish tanks, and the fish is what you've come for.

A smell of cologne preceded the arrival at the table of Mr Liu, the owner, who was a farmer before he had a spell working in construction. How he ended up running one of the city's most exclusive restaurants and becoming an expert in the famous river fish of the region was a question he didn't get around to answering but he did cast a glance at his smart Rolex watch at the time of asking. Outside there was a line of Japanese cars with darkened windows and the private rooms were nearly all booked out tonight. He makes, said Mr Liu, about RMB1 million per year, but things aren't what they were a couple of years back. He kept using the word 'recession'.

'The system is getting more perfect,' explained Kin-wai's cousin, an air-conditioning agent responsible for fitting out Beijing's Olympic Village. He said it without a trace of irony. 'People are earning less, they're finding fewer ways to get more money — so they're spending less money in restaurants.' Days were when no table would spend less than RMB1,000 to maintain face; now people are far more practical and Mr Liu has been forced to drop some of his prices. Turtle he used to sell at RMB250 per catty (600 grammes) but now he can't charge much more than RMB70. Having said that, he had with apparent confidence secured that night a two-foot long turtle which he said would fetch him RMB1,500 and provide a table of twelve with a delicious soup and another turtle dish of their choice. Dinner for three that night cost RMB130 for six excellent fish dishes including a melt-in-your mouth sole and a huge plate of freshwater prawns; a quality impossible to find in Zhuhai City where the price would, in any event, be at least twice as high. Kin-wai's cousin insisted on paying. He couldn't welcome two visitors to his home town and expect them to entertain either him or themselves. It is an attitude, often rather embarrassing to a Westerner, which occurs time and time again in this most hospitable of countries.

Zhongshan is famous for its river fish; Shunde has traditionally nurtured the top Cantonese chefs and used to be famous for all kinds of delicacies; today it is known principally for something extremely un-Cantonese, and that is milk. Shunde is another hour north of Zhongshan City, and is probably the most prosperous city in the whole of Guangdong Province, still benefitting from its days as a centre of the lucrative silk trade. The presence of this trade meant that women were born into the reality of economic independence; it is no coincidence therefore that Shunde is also the original home of free-thinking young women who early this century chose, in preference to becoming the property of a husband in whom they had not a flicker of interest, to go into service. They became known as the 'black and white' amahs so revered in cities like Singapore and Hong Kong where they offered a quality of service unmatched by any other group or nationality, then or since.

In Shunde the Portuguese influence is seen not in colonial architecture as in Zhongshan but in dishes unknown to any other city in the province — and that is principally what Kin-wai had brought me there for. Milk dishes are clearly the result of some Western influence given that the Chinese do not traditionally eat any dairy products; they even have a less-than-flattering description for Caucasians in terms of what they detect as an unpleasant body odour resulting, they'll say, from eating too many dairy products.

The restaurant inside the walls of the historic Chinese garden in Shunde, Qing Hui Yuan, is the most popular restaurant in town and the second most expensive, at least according to the taxi driver. Groups of ladies-that-lunch and pairs of businessmen occupied the

Shellfish, Zhuhai

best window tables overlooking the garden, though the garden was a mess of construction of modern features like an ugly fountain. Traditional roofs were coming down and one can only hope the tiles will be cleaned and recycled rather than thrown away. No one at lunch paid much attention to the garden, now commercialised and rather sad, and merrily mixed their Dynasty red wine with 7-Up. The market for red wine in China is booming, to the delight of the French in particular, but producers would shudder to see this practice, even if it were being conducted with wine produced in Tianjin rather than something from Bordeaux. Purists might dismiss this practice as something akin to putting sugar in tea or milk in coffee; after all, they're just making a version of sangria. But when Sandy Leong, Macau wine merchant, is entertaining in China, she painstakingly instructs waiting staff that those mixing their red wine with lemonade don't get the Chateau Latour 1982, they get the cheap French stuff.

Qing Hui Yuan restaurant serves 'flaming milk', to make which the kitchen mixes milk with preserved sausage, nuts and egg white and cooks it in a piping-hot wok. The method of cooking is home-style, the dish is cheap to make, yet the result is a rich and extremely satisfying dish. That's the salted version. The taxi driver said that, for for an extra RMB20, would drive us almost to the door of the famous restaurant in Shunde where they make sweet milk dishes, so a deal was again struck. Having a car wait outside while you eat dessert seemed a civilised, Shunde kind of thing to do. The cold set milk puddings and warm creamy ones, taken with tea in an old-fashioned little shop with traditional tea-shop tables and chairs and a marvellously leisured atmosphere, were clearly Portuguese in inspiration. Both dishes tasted and looked similar to the Portuguese-inspired desserts that can be tasted in Macau in a little restaurant on the Largo do Senado, Leitaria I Son, today frequented almost exclusively by Chinese. China introduced the West to rhubarb; it seems a fair exchange.

A gentle stroll down Foshan's main street — too gentle for me, really; I believe we get less tired when we walk faster — and I was learning a great deal. He Jin drinks Portuguese wine brought back for him by

Chapter 4: The west side

friends visiting Macau and he prefers it, he said, to French wine. He Jin reads books about Chinese history and culture which he borrows from his brother's huge collection. He knows and likes good food, he has a sensitivity to art and calligraphy, nurtured by an artistic father, and loves landscapes which offer mountains, trees and waterfalls. And he enthuses about British culture, surfing the Internet to find out more about pop band The Spice Girls whom he has seen on satellite television, and British soccer is his other thing; Newcastle United is his favourite team. He Jin's big new interest is Mauritius, information about which he's also searching for on the Internet. He knows it is beautiful, that South Africa honeymoons there, that it has easy access to many countries in Africa, and that its population is made up of people of mostly Chinese and Indian descent.

His interest in Mauritius is very specific and not a flight of fancy. The day I met him, He Jin was expecting to hear at any moment whether or not his employer in the prosperous city of Foshan, the Shiwan Economic & Industries General Company, for which he works in the international trade department, was sending him to Mauritius to work in the overseas office. He told me, as if this was an exceptional practice, that he would be able to take with him Deng Shun, his wife of one year. Deng Shun is a sweet and attractive young woman employed in a job for which she has the perfect personality — in the front office of the three-star Foshan Overseas Chinese Hotel, the second best hotel in the city after the four-star Foshan Hotel. When the two fell in love, He Jin told me, he began to make frequent gifts of roses, her favourite flower — and he hasn't stopped making such gifts today. They make an appealing couple. Confident and capable, interested and interesting, it is not difficult to understand why He Jin's employer should consider him, at twenty-eight years old, a young man of great promise with a great future and so consider him for this posting.

Driving down from Guangzhou one day, I had wandered into the Foshan Overseas Chinese Hotel to call up a friend of a friend who had said he'd love to meet me and show me around. The girls in the hotel's business centre were extremely friendly but even their help did not succeed in locating this mystery man. Keen to look around the city with another pair of eyes than just my own, and always preferring to eat lunch in company rather than alone, if only to be able to try more dishes, I asked at reception if they could organise me a guide. I was talking to Deng Shun, who said she could certainly help. I was asked to wait for twenty minutes, during which time we fell into conversation. The guide, it turned out, was to be her husband on an extended lunch break.

For the breadth of subjects He Jin was able to talk about, it was his knowledge of and love for Foshan which dominated. He's remarkably well travelled throughout China, and can still only conclude that Foshan is the most comfortable city in which to live in the whole country. He moved to Foshan two years ago from his home town of Nanjing, where he graduated in computer science, sent by his company to work at Headquarters. A year later he returned to Nanjing to marry Deng Chun, and he brought her back to the city with him. She too loves it.

At the start, he confessed, it was not easy to integrate, but now he was feeling very accepted, and although his native Mandarin could easily suffice in Guangdong Province, he learnt Cantonese and not only that, he learnt it in just three months — which is roughly the time it took his wife to learn it, too. 'Perhaps we have a facility in language learning,' he said. The pair live in 109 square metres for which they pay just RMB60, he enthused, imparting this information without prompt. If he was a manager, that would be more like 150 square metres. The city is clean, it is not crowded, and he enjoys his lifestyle. Number One issue for He is to have enough money to live a comfortable life, but he is actually more interested in the comfortable life than the money if that distinction is valid: he has many hobbies, he told me, such as photography and he wants to be free to pursue them. No interest in politics, he confirmed; no interest at all in who is governing the country. So long as he can lead the kind of life he wants to lead. And he can do that in Foshan.

He Jin and Deng Chun are not alone in their enthusiasm. Foshan is where people love to live, whether they're born and bred there or

Chapter 4: The west side

hail from another province. The future of Guangdong Province lies not in Guangzhou but thirty minutes away in Foshan, its most forthright supporters will tell you. Foshan has everything Guangzhou has — minus the dirty air and the historical baggage.

It certainly does appear that if Guangzhou had any exclusive suburbs, Foshan would be the most sophisticated and middle-class of them all. The only area much like Foshan you can find in Guangzhou is the area of Tianhebeilu in the north-east of the city, but this is conceived to become the new downtown rather than a smart suburb. Site of the sparkling new railway station (official launch date: 1 July, 1997), the shiny new office buildings and residential towers rise from its wide streets and have been planned with space around them and leisure facilities and parks between them. Yet Tianhebeilu cannot escape the density of human movement, the noise and the volume of traffic which besets the city of Guangzhou at every hour. In Foshan people can cross half-empty streets without risking the ire or ineptitude of a taxi driver. Hardly a car hoots its horn. What's more, residents can comfortably walk along streets because the pavements are wide and do not have to be shared with hundreds of other people, and they're level and properly paved with coloured or patterned tiles.

Foshan's most extreme contrast to Guangzhou is in the air quality. Not only are the pavements pleasant to walk on, the air is clean enough to be breathed. The roads which lead to shopping centres, hotels and office towers are tree-lined. Even the periphery has a sense of order about it. Roadside timber yards clean up around themselves, trucks with interesting loads like ceramic planters pass by, and there might even be a pair of water buffalo safely sharing the same road. Pylons stretch into the distance, a single, thin chimney emits a stream of dark smoke, and a single, ugly industrial building billows white smoke — but this is the total pollution to be seen. Residential towers are in blue or pink, reminiscent of the Hong Kong new towns Shatin and Tuen Mun. New roads and new overpasses are going up before they're needed — Highway 321 is a vast and empty road here in Foshan — rather than as some form of transport crisis management. Construction workers miraculously clear up after themselves, too.

Chapter 4: The west side

Foshan looks more like a Special Economic Zone than one of the officially-designated SEZS, but the essence of its aesthetic and soulful appeal is to be found in the attending sense of culture and history which necessarily elude the conglomerations which have built up in Shenzhen or Zhuhai. Foshan has plenty of handsome, modern buildings but it also happens to be one of China's three oldest cities, governed by an administration which is taking an active role in the preservation of the old city. 'Thinking about temples, thinking of Shunde and Nanhai' (Foshan was formerly part of Nanhai) is a famous saying, and this preponderance of temples had much to do with the profusion of different industries in the area. Each industry, whether iron or handicrafts or textiles or commerce had a designated temple as its 'guild'. Foshan itself never had much tradition in agriculture, causing it to develop other forms of income. Although no longer famous for exquisite porcelain, it is today known for ceramic tiles for use both in the exterior and interiors of buildings. There are few handicrafts these days but the garment industry produces at the high quality end. Other important industries include electronics and light bulbs.

Foshan has, together with prosperous cities throughout the Pearl River Delta, attracted workers from neighbouring provinces, but it is a large enough city in its own right to fill many of its own jobs, providing a tighter cohesion among workers who have a shared heritage. In any case, incoming workers have tended to be higher skilled professionals like He Jin and his wife. While old cities like Guangzhou and new towns like Shenzhen watch in varying states of despair the daily influx from the Guangdong countryside or from other provinces, hoping to make their fortune or even just find a job, Foshan has been spared the resulting social problems of quite what to do with all those who fit the profile of unskilled farmers from the poor north-east of Guangdong Province.

One of the most impressive new buildings in Foshan is the green-glassed Baihua Plaza, at fifty-three stories the city's tallest office tower. The building sits proudly on a street corner and has such stores as Esprit, Watson's and Kentucky Fried Chicken at street level. Cross

Temple, Foshan

the street and after a two-minute stroll you are at the gates of the city's oldest building, Foshan Zu Miao, or Ancestry Temple, which counts as the heart of the city and remains tremendously important to the population. At Chinese New Year, it is difficult to even get within the sprawling compound, and the central pond, in the middle of which crouches a stone turtle with a stone snake wrapped around it, fills to overflowing with coins in as little as four hours. The custom is to throw a coin in the hope that it will hit the turtle's head and good luck will follow. Construction of the temple began in 1078 during the Song dynasty (960–1279) and though much of the original was tragically burnt down, rebuilding began as soon as 1372 at the beginning of the Ming dynasty. For formal or informal students of architecture, its design is of immense interest in the way it bears direct reference to *Rules of Architecture,* a book dating to the Song dynasty.

Crucially, the temple has grown with the city, and the continual upgrading and development of the area is a compelling illustration of the way in which Foshan has been able to continually reinvent itself over the decades and even centuries. In this must lie its success. It is the same story at the famous Liang's Garden, one of Guangdong's most famous scholar's gardens which reflects the abiding cultural importance of Foshan. The Liang family remains an important family in Southeast Asia, known last century throughout the region for the skills of four family members who were masters in poetry, painting and calligraphy. Much of the garden dates to the early 1800s but it fell into major decay after 1949. The Foshan government began work on restoring the garden in 1982, declared it a protected zone, and returned not only its residences and ancestral temples to their former glory, but created new gardens areas, bridges and waterways within its extended walls.

He Jin found me a taxi in which I could return to Guangzhou, and I said my farewells to Deng Shun inside the hotel as staff are not allowed to leave by the main entrance. She asked if she could write to me. The deal He Jin finalised with the taxi driver was actually a figure higher than the meter fare I'd paid in the morning from the White Swan, but He Jin believed he had saved me some money.

Chapter 4: The west side

Whatever the price, I was happy not to have to pick up a taxi myself. There is always this nagging worry, not knowing the roads, as to whether I'm actually getting taken to the place I've asked to be dropped at. Perhaps this makes eventually arriving at that destination all the more rewarding. Positive travel experience is not seeing a temple and doing a smart foreign exchange deal on the street, but about getting somewhere you want to go; in this case in the world's most populated and perhaps most foreign country. This I concluded as I lowered myself onto the tatty back seat.

Chapter 5: The east side

Zhao yen is eighteen years old. Shy and pretty with slightly pink cheeks, she was born in Sichuan Province and, six months ago, moved to Shenzhen at the suggestion of her brother who works at a joint-venture Japanese factory producing electronic components. She works as a waitress in the top Sichuan restaurant in a building called Sichuan Tower and speaks Mandarin but no Cantonese. Today, a Tuesday, inexplicably in a community so economically reformed, the building's ground-floor supermarkets which sell all kinds of unusual peppers and chillies and other food items from Sichuan, were shut for stock-taking. 'Probably government-owned,' said my food advisor for the day, Hong Kong gourmet Lau Kin-wai, who reckons this is the best Sichuan restaurant in Shenzhen.

For someone like me whose interest in travel begins with exploring the local cuisine and searching out good food, followed by scratching beneath the surface to discover something about individual people and culture (so much the better if they're combined in conversations over the dinner table), Kin-wai is the best guide. Besides knowing food, he'll chat to anyone, anywhere, and ask the kind of questions others might consider impolite but which he delivers with such aplomb that people can't help but respond. Broader cultural preoccupations are to my mind very important in much of China where, even if a city has one tourist attraction, the rest is probably bereft of overt appeal. You have to create your own interest. In a society which takes its food very seriously, if you can eat the local food with the locals, you're halfway to discovering the culture; indeed you're physically partaking of it.

Kin-wai explained briefly how Sichuan Province is very poor, how its best exports are its food and its people, which well explains why so many Sichuan restaurants can be found outside the province. I took the thought on a little, concluding that Sichuan food, with its distinctive peppery flavours and chilli hot finishes, is an esoteric taste;

it is also considered a rustic cuisine. A Cantonese restaurant in Sichuan's capital city of Chengdu, on the other hand, would probably be the most prestigious and expensive restaurant in town, because the food of Guangdong is famed not only for the quality of its ingredients, particularly fish and seafood, but for the lightness of touch in its preparation and cooking. No other Chinese cooking style is so fine.

In the second-floor restaurant Zhao Yen earns RMB500 per month, an amount which might buy her a couple of lunches with her brother were she the customer. At home she would earn no more than RMB300, and that is if she could find a job. Even though RMB500 may not be vastly more than she could earn in Sichuan, the point is that she is now living minutes from Hong Kong and she has been completely seduced by what she imagines it is like. In reality, like the majority of Shenzhen's population, she is unlikely to ever visit the place. 'Can you find me a rich husband in Hong Kong?' she asked Kin-wai. Her colleague poured water into the teacup from a kettle with a two foot long spout. 'What is the significance of pouring water from such a kettle,' I asked, 'how does it improve the quality of the tea?' She looked worried. Sorry, she didn't know, she had only started the day before. Or failing a husband, Zhao Yen continued, she would love to get a job in Hong Kong — and get rich. In reality, if she landed in Hong Kong, she would likely end up under the control of an underground society and waitressing would be a polite word for what she would be doing. Even in Shenzhen she's lucky that, as a peasant girl from the north, she is working in a reputable restaurant.

In Chinese they call Shenzhen 'the immigrant city'. Little surprise if you consider that just seventeen years ago when it was conferred with the title 'Special Economic Zone' its population was 30,000, now risen to four million. Easily the most successful SEZ, when compared with Zhuhai and Shantou in Guangdong Province, or Hainan Island and Xiamen, it was here more than almost anywhere in China where, on the Memorial Day of Deng Xiaoping, businessmen and market makers paused to remember the man whom they consider made it all possible. By day's end, the downtown hoarding bearing Deng's

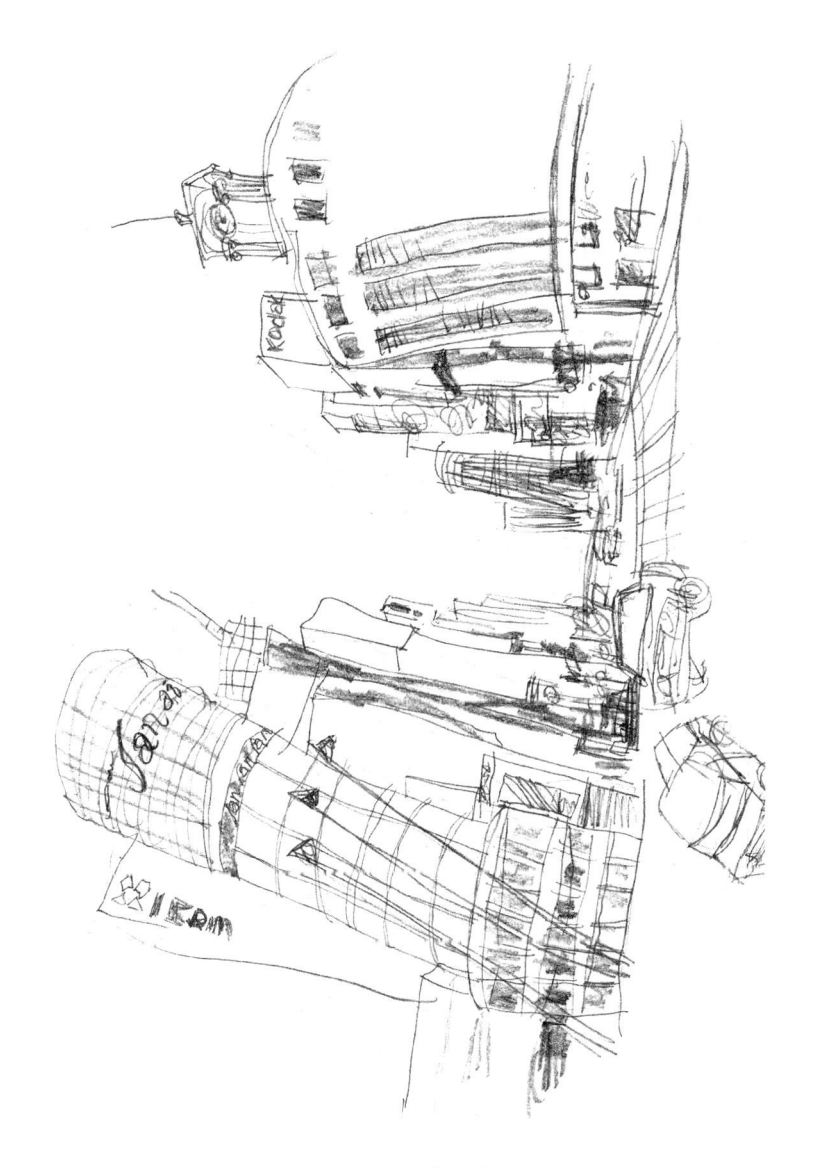

Downtown, Shenzhen

portrait was hanging above a mass of scattered flowers, and thousands of people had bowed before it. If people weren't rich yet, they knew that Shenzhen at least promised the possibility of wealth.

The development of the SEZ began west of Shenzhen itself in Shekou, a deep-sea port with a more than one-hundred-year history in shipping and ship-building and excellent relationships with Hong Kong. It's a forty-five-minute run from the port area to downtown which more than anything indicates the magnitude of the zone. In many ways Shekou is more pleasant than downtown: the port may not be shiny and new but it has been renovated, and the industrial area surrounding it comprises smart, modern buildings set along tree-lined avenues with well-tended flower beds at their centre. The roads are wide and while Shenzhen does not share the sense of openness and clean air quality of Zhuhai, neither does its infrastructure suffer with the ugliness and grime of areas just north of its own border in the direction of Dongguan. Downtown, the busy border, the bus station, the rows of little shops and local residents touting all kinds of business on the street from money changing to endangered animals, create a disorder at odds with the calm of Shekou but perfectly befitting a city whose citizens know no bounds when it comes to market forces. Yet to plan and develop a new city which works smoothly and caters consistently well to a population which has necessarily exploded, is something of a modern miracle — or an urban nightmare, depending on how you choose to look at it.

Some of Hong Kong's pace and energy can be felt on Shenzhen streets. Still, Shenzhen is a wannabe Hong Kong without the style, the overseas influence and the international acclaim which have made the SAR such a world power. Shiny buildings go up in a loosely Hong Kong style, but the details are strange enough to suggest such buildings are largely designed by architects lacking a rounded education or any real exposure to world trends. They are then built by construction companies with such a scant regard for the quality of execution that once the essentials are done, all else is forgotten. Caring only about the minimum, no attention is paid to finishings or to boundaries;

piles of rubble and sand are left to fester; and frills like curbs on pavements are ignored. All this results in a downtown mess.

The city's leisure facilities are meanwhile nothing but curious in their conception. As if defensive about its lack of a past or a culture it can call its own, Shenzhen authorities have erected bizarre theme parks like China Folk Culture Villages and the neighbouring Splendid China which, besides featuring scale models of some of China's most famous buildings and presenting China village folk culture, has also commissioned similarly proportioned models of Europe's most famous landmarks such as the Eiffel Tower. To see a row of faux-nineteenth-century European houses in downtown Shenzhen does indeed suggest you are in a city which doesn't know if it is coming or going.

The leisure activity which works particularly well in Shenzhen is eating. Huge immigrant groups bring the cuisine of their own province with them, and almost every branch of Chinese cooking can be experienced to a high quality in this city. Close to the border with Hong Kong you can buy a roast goose for HK$35 from a Shenzhen trader which in Hong Kong would cost you HK$120, but eat in a fancy restaurant with cachet for the wealthy Taiwanese or Hong Kong businessman: open kitchen, the freshest seafood from waters close by, plenty of red wine (even if the staff have no idea how to open a bottle), and you pay at least what you'd pay in a Hong Kong hotel restaurant. You know of course that quite a bit of that bill will end up with your guide in commission, though it is hardly a practice unique to Shenzhen. I refuse to get used to it, though. The other thing I refuse to get used to but may have to give in to eventually is the rigid mentality of the typical guide. However often I say that I am not a normal visitor, neither tourist nor businesswoman, that I have far more interest in the sounds than the sights of a city, I am introduced to restaurants for tourists and taken into grubby little souvenir shops.

People from outside the province who now live and work in Shenzhen purport to dislike the lack of lifestyle it offers. They say it is a terrible place in which to bring up a family, they despise its overt money-making ethos, its lack of friendliness and its lack of culture. But they have no interest in wider political issues and they too are there, thinking up new and clever ways to make money — this is surely the most important part of Shenzhen culture — like renting out their houses while themselves living in dormitories. Even his bell boys, says the chief concierge of an international hotel in the city, have been able to buy a house, though he thinks he could personally make at least as much money as he earns in Shenzhen back in his home city of Beijing these days.

Across the street from that same hotel barefoot children who cannot be aged more than ten carry a tiny baby under one arm and a begging bowl under the other. So expert are they, particularly when they see someone who is clearly from the Hong Kong side of the border, they'll almost push you into the road until you've parted with some money. Middle ground between sentimentality and cynicism is hard to find, but a glance behind probably reveals somewhere in the distance the triad member who controls this particular street and he's keeping his eye on how well the child is doing. 'Cross the street!' suggested a helpful and be-suited local and sure enough it worked. But across that road we came face to face with another Shenzhen phenomenon. Dozens and dozens of prostitutes, women from all over China, drinking coffees in a hotel lobby, waiting to dine in the same hotel's expensive Cantonese restaurant with clients.

It is estimated, and on this people from both sides of the border concur, that two out of three males travelling from Hong Kong to Shenzhen are visiting a mistress. It is an age-old practice in Chinese culture but increasingly unacceptable to Hong Kong wives, who now have support groups and counsellors specialising in the phenomenon. An outlay of some HK$3,000 per month allows a man to put up a woman in an apartment, an outlay which back home in Hong Kong would hardly secure him an hour in Club BBoss. There are plenty of things Hongkongers like to buy in China but in Shenzhen women are clearly the most popular product. At the border of Hong Kong and Shenzhen, you don't see men with the packs of toilet rolls and bags of vegetables which cross from Zhuhai into Macau.

On ordinary days up to 100,000 Hongkongers cross the border from Lo Wu, Hong Kong's most northerly point, into the mayhem which is Shenzhen; at Chinese New Year it is a terrifying two million. Exiting Hong Kong was always smooth, even in the crowds, but Shenzhen was a claustrophobic nightmare until they opened the smart new border building controlled by computers. If you don't have connections and thus don't have a VIP card, and cannot use the express channel, it can still take up to two hours — half-an-hour on the quietest Tuesday morning — to finally get into China. Crossing the bridge through no-man's land over the Shenzhen River takes five minutes. For some people, like Kin-wai's mother, it takes an inexplicable twenty years. Or it becomes the unrequited wish of a lifetime. Shenzhen dreams of Hong Kong, even though the majority of residents have still never smelt the city for themselves, and even after reunification, border control remains its same restrictive self.

Shenzhen's special relationship to Hong Kong, its craving to be Hong Kong, is all the more apparent from the ferry, and that's the ferry from Zhuhai. During office hours it runs four times an hour — the link between Macau and Shenzhen, or between Hong Kong and Zhuhai, amounts to just one boat a day — and at a quarter to ten on a Sunday morning the catamaran was full. The tour groups were given away by their matching caps, matching bags and matching dialects, but in between all that purple and green there were plenty of serious looking business types rather than families going out for lunch or to visit one of Shenzhen's more bizarre tourist attractions. Moving out of Zhuhai's orderly new ferry terminal just out of town, not twenty minutes had passed before the city had transformed into a fuzzy outline. This particular time slot was served by a boat with a first class upper deck which, for an upgrade of RMB20 on the standard RMB65, in addition to a free bottle of mineral water allowed passengers the rather pleasant experience of getting out on deck.

The careless eye, viewing from a distance, could imagine the catamaran was about to dock in Hong Kong. Topographically, climatically, for soil types, flora and fauna, Shenzhen may as well be Hong Kong. Borders are, after all, political. It takes minutes for the waters of the Pearl River Delta which lap alongside the shore at Shekou to reach Hong Kong's Tsing Yi container terminal. The same waters which, before the ceding of Hong Kong and subsequently the Kowloon Peninsula from the Chinese to the British, were skilfully circumnavigated by skippers. Little can have changed since then. The boats out on the waters of the Shekou harbour may be smaller and more modern than those which provided the backdrop to the Opium Wars, but the chimneys and the dark peaks of small islands with pagodas and temples at their summits remain the same and of course the sea itself, though today more polluted, retains the same omniscience. Hong Kong's eminence in this delta is distinctly felt — here one is on the Chinese waters of the Pearl River Delta but the Hong Kong signals for mobile phone users are strong. Exerting control out on the water is more difficult than on land, as the Chinese too late discovered in their tragic underestimation of the strength of the British navy.

That ferry service linking the SEZ of the eastern side of the Pearl River Delta with the SEZ of the western side circumvents Hong Kong and reinforces Shenzhen's position as the very pinnacle of progressive business environments on the mainland. Shenzhen's attitude to Hong Kong is perfectly mirrored in the way that most of China regards Shenzhen. The success of Shenzhen specifically relates to its proximity to Hong Kong — the Hong Kong dollar is a second, official currency here — but Zhuhai is not Macau's equivalent to Hong Kong's Shenzhen. While Shenzhen emulates Hong Kong, so Zhuhai emulates Shenzhen and barely spares Macau a thought, except if it wants to eat Portuguese *bacalhau* (salted codfish) and drink Dao 1984. Zhuhai cadres look not to Macau for know-how and resources but to Shenzhen. Beijing also looks to Shenzhen, regarding it as a city of great political significance; a notional though hardly geographical halfway house between Beijing and Hong Kong. It proves, they are saying, how Deng's 'one country two systems' policy can be put to work in Hong Kong. For within China's pre–July 1997 borders there is a city called Shenzhen which fosters very different working practices and very different motivations to the rest of the country.

There are problems too. For all its obvious successes, an enormous disparity in wealth, as exists in so many cities around the world, has

Chapter 5: The east side

in this special economic zone developed to epic proportions in less than a decade. Many Hong Kong and Macau-Chinese refuse to visit the SEZ, so concerned are they for their personal safety. Besides the more obvious examples of begging children, most of the city's workers live dormitory style with up to six per room, and those occupying management positions share basic apartments. Deng's economic miracle, analysts are saying, could result in unprecedented social problems as citizens understand first hand the principle of letting a few people get rich first. If you've begun your professional life under a communist system which espouses equality, how are you supposed to get your mind around inequality, especially when it is you who is less equal than your neighbour?

'Don't take a mini-bus north,' advised the restaurant manager at the Sichuan restaurant, 'it is too dangerous.' Buses could get stopped in a secluded spot by armed highwaymen and all the passengers robbed. Such roads are not even safe for locals, with stories commonplace of young local men riding motorbikes being shot and the motorbike stolen. 'Far better to take a taxi,' the manager said, and in a gesture in complete contrast to the robbers he was describing, sent out one of his waiters to secure a good price. 'The journey should cost about RMB50,' said the waiter, though he was clearly a bit out of touch and the cheapest offer was RMB230. Egged on by Kin-wai's questions, the taxi driver grumbled about business being bad and he was clearly unhappy to drive us to Dongguan, uncertain if he would be able to find a fare back to the zone. He was protected in the front seat by a wire cage. It is interesting to note which cities in the Pearl River Delta — places like Foshan and Shunde — do not require their cab drivers to cage themselves in.

The road which leads out of Shenzhen in the direction of Dongguan City, halfway to Guangzhou, at first recedes into the gutters and is extremely busy with laden trucks and dusty buses as well as smart cars and foreign-made motorbikes. Later it develops into a fast and efficient four-lane highway bordered by steep slopes planted with terraces of vegetables. Women sell bunches of bananas at toll booths.

Chapter 5: The east side

Surreal buildings which house multi-purpose entertainment centres appear out of nowhere; a Disneyland vision with turrets and towers and arches which exist outside time as well as outside a typical, contemporary understanding of the relationship between form and space. They tell a story of a fairy-tale life and provide an extraordinary contrast to the monotony of grey industrial buildings which surround them. This eastern side of the Pearl River Delta is altogether an unpleasant area to look at. Compared to the west, this area is agriculturally poor, its vegetation sparse, its unfinished buildings and deserted building sites many.

Main cities on the east side like Dongguan and Huizhou are ugly, polluted conglomerations burdened with ugly, grime-covered 1950s industrial buildings; outdated testaments to the communist regime. People go to Dongguan City to visit historic gardens dating to 1850 where intellectuals would gather in the past, or to try *lap cheong*, a Chinese sausage which is particularly good here during the winter months when humidity is low and it can dry properly, though how anything dried in Dongguan City's air can be eaten is a puzzle. Huizhou City boasts a West Lake, designed after Hangzhou's identically named tourist attraction, but it is unfortunately bereft of the latter's size or romance.

There are few other obvious reasons to visit such cities, but what makes them so successful, the reason they attract so many businessmen, is something decidedly unromantic. That is, proximity to Shenzhen. Operating as overspills where land and labour are cheaper, they are Shenzhen without the shiny office towers and self-made entrepreneurs checking their pagers and making calls on their mobile phones in smart hotel lobbies. They similarly attract scores of workers from outside Guangdong and foster a climate in which money can be made. Something else in their favour, and indeed this applies to many towns and villages across the Pearl River Delta, is the fact that many overseas Chinese or Hong Kong-ese or their families were born there and through existing connections they choose to invest in the city of their ancestors. A large proportion of American Chinese, for example, come from the city of Taishan on the west side, and they all send back money. Taishan prospers. In the case of Dongguan City, others with no particular familial links to the city have made similar decisions, for them based purely on economics. Mr Cheung, for example, left his family and his beautiful home city of Zhaoqing to set up a printing factory here. He traded quality of life for standard of living and his standard of living is now impressively high.

We didn't even get her name, but the young woman Kin-wai engaged in conversation was not shy to discuss the particulars of her life in Dongguan City. Today, in the company of her proud parents, she was visiting Hoi Yuan, Dongguan's famous gardens, and the family members were taking endless photographs of each other, soliciting other visitors to take pictures of the three of them together. Ask a young woman like her how much she earns and she's delighted to respond in great detail. She had been living in the city, she said, for five years now, leaving home to seek work, and had recently been promoted. She now earned RMB1,100 per month, most of which she sent home to her farming parents who live near Laoyin in Hunan Province, former capital of the Tang dynasty. She made an additional RMB150 by writing, and this freelance wage was the money she was basically living on. Smartly dressed and confident, this bright young woman was a vivid contrast to her parents on their first adventure away from their home village. They rarely see Caucasians and asked to have their photograph taken with me.

Hearing about young women chatting so openly about money sounds strange to people from Western cultures, where money is one of the most common causes of arguments between married couples, but is, paradoxically, considered an impolite and crass subject. Where living is still about survival, money is the number one commodity, the number one way to a better life. Every young person in China knows that a bicycle costs RMB500, that a Japanese motorcycle costs RMB30,000 but that a locally made one costs RMB10,000, that even without buying a car it costs RMB200,000 to keep it on the road per year.

The taxi driver hadn't known the way to the gardens of Hoi Yuan and pulled in to ask a man on a motorcycle for directions. He said he would show the way for RMB20, a fee which would of course be paid by the passenger and not the driver. That was bargained down to RMB10 but it was a lovely illustration of how no one in this city is going to miss a trick; they're certainly not going to give directions for free. People mill about on street corners as if they're waiting for just such golden little opportunities to arrive in their palms. And this being Guangdong, there is plenty of gold to go around.

WISH YOU HAVE A PLEASANT JOURNEY was written on a signboard at the dirty, northernmost toll gate out of Dongguan, and within minutes, drab factories stretching far into the horizon, the car had hit the suburban sprawl of Guangzhou, its centre still an hour away.

Chapter 6: Zhaoqing, the scenic spot

WITH EVERY SEAT FULL, as usual, the 6AM jetfoil from Macau to Hong Kong felt like a boat leaving an inaccessible corner of interior China where the women stay at home and the men do whatever it is that men do when they get together in bonded little groups. Rather than the usually cosmopolitan crowd travelling during quieter and more conventional times of the day, this was a curiously threatening group, almost entirely Chinese men aged between thirty and forty, all no doubt trying to get back to Hong Kong in time for as hard a day at the office as they would be able to manage. One guy with a three-inch long nail on the little finger of his left hand (all the better for counting money, my dear) flicked through a thick wad of crisp HK$500 notes with the intensity of a bank teller, and laughed and joked with his friends. He was feeling generous. The duty-free cartons of Salem Lights ordered by his three travelling companions were on him.

Not every gambler leaves with wads of notes that thick and many lose wads that thick; it was clear in any case that almost everyone on the boat had been trying their luck at Macau's myriad tables. The majority slept — how enviable is that ability to sleep anywhere, anytime — hoping that fifty or so minutes would see them through the day. Just before arrival in the choppy waters of Hong Kong's Victoria Harbour, most opened the red box given to first-class passengers and took out the characterless Macey's muffin and the heart-shaped low quality milk chocolate. Some got up and went to the machine at the front of the boat to make themselves a paper cup of instant coffee with powder creamer; an attempt to give them a kick in their step and make it efficiently to Sheung Wan MTR station.

If that boat journey felt like an alien, China experience, leaving on the 8:10AM catamaran from Tsimshatsui bound for Zhaoqing from the terminal in the basement of the glossy gold China Hong Kong City was even more extraordinary. Quieter during the rest of the day with few boats arriving or departing en masse, more than a dozen boats leave at this pre-breakfast hour for destinations like Shekou, Zhuhai, Lianhuashan, Tai Ping and various other ports in the Pearl River Delta which even travel agents don't seem to know about, not even when they have a timetable in front of them. New routes are added almost as frequently as new golf courses are opened up the delta, but still the terminal does not reach twenty-four-hour capacity.

The closer it gets to a public holiday (Chinese New Year is the busiest time, of course) the more out-of-control the crowd of travellers becomes, but even on this pre–Easter Tuesday securing a ticket required nerves of steel and a complete rejection of the notions of good manners and orderly queues. The pushing and shoving at the ticket office here is surpassed only by the behaviour of customers at the old Guangzhou Railway Station. I'm embarrassed, particularly in front of visiting Westerners, to see myself pushing and swearing along with the swell, barely stepping aside for women and children. Cultural appropriation, survival, straightforward bad manners... who knows, but if you need a ticket fast, as I did, there is no time to ponder those questions. Travel experiences like these mean my reactions to the London Underground, a paradigm of standing aside and letting the passengers off first, please, have to be quickly and severely modified when I arrive in England.

Once through passport control, there seems to be little relationship between the signposted 'waiting areas' and the jetties from which each boat will eventually leave, but the idea is not to take the signs too literally. A ferry terminal like this might be large enough to cope with crowds, but it could never have imagined offering boats to so many destinations. There really is a system, and a monitor, and the simple technique is to remain calm at all times including during pre-boarding procedures, and not just in the unlikely event of a catastrophe at sea. To go from Macau to Hong Kong to Zhaoqing before lunch was unlikely to be anything but a demanding experience, particularly after four hours of rather low-grade sleep.

Music blared out from the catamaran's speakers, the kind of music that used to be played on myriad streets in China over the public address system. There was luggage everywhere, children played with new Hong Kong toys in the aisles, and the women's washroom was denoted by a little figure with pigtails. The feeling of being in China before the catamaran had even pulled out of Hong Kong, what with the China-style crush and the numbers of mainland Chinese returning home with huge bags stuffed with shopping, echoed the sensation of two hours earlier that the jetfoil was leaving not Macau but China. It was clearly an illusion. The sensation did however nicely confirm that China as it exists in the mind, and it exists very powerfully in most minds, is a complex and very personal set of expectations to be either exceeded, met or crushed, for good or for bad.

This ferry journey to China had effectively began the night before when I received a telephone call during a delicious and extravagant dinner of wild boar and guinea fowl in the Hotel Lisboa's upmarket A Galera restaurant in Macau. The call advised me not to go. A week earlier, splashed on the front pages of all local newspapers, we had read about the accidental tipping of 200 barrels of cyanide into the Gui River on the west side of the Pearl River Delta. Water provision in Macau was immediately transferred to a reservoir with a forty-day supply while the extent of the problem was assessed. Heavy rains just north of the Macau border quickly diluted the poison, the driver of the lorry carrying the fifty-kilogramme barrels was charged with negligence, and the whole thing blew over. But now I was hearing from a friend in Hong Kong, whose cousin lived in Zhaoqing, that Zhaoqing was the worst affected city in Guangdong. I should be unable to eat any food that had even been near water, he said. Having survived a bout of cholera contracted in Vietnam I was not about to change any travelling plans on account of water. He continued by saying that travelling alone in a taxi in the region might not be safe. Still not hearing from me what he wanted he gave up and said I was brave. He also told me that his cousin would meet me in the city at the Dynasty Hotel to introduce me to a guide.

All this telephone to-ing and fro-ing was punctuated by the rather surreal stopping and starting of a film crew from TDM, Macau's own television channel, who were putting together a seven-minute slot for the breakfast show about a day in the life of the dinner's host, Sandy

Leong. Would that every night brought a dinner and wines of that calibre. Sandy has her own wine business and brought along three Pomerols she was considering adding to her portfolio for the mixed gathering of Portuguese, British, Chinese and Macanese to taste. The discussion was conducted in English, with Sandy taking on the difficult task of translating for the camera into Cantonese; difficult because developing a vocabulary for describing wine in Chinese is still a relatively new pursuit. When those bottles were finished, Filipe Santos, chairman of the Macau Wine Society, ordered a bottle of La Conseillante 1992 which came in at a very competitive 1,100 Macau patacas. A Galera has the best wine list in Macau thanks to Alan Ho, nephew to Macau's king of gambling, Dr Stanley Ho. Alan Ho personally looks after the hotel's wine list, buying at auction in London and, even better, refusing to mark the wines up threefold, which given the high duty in Asia can create ludicrous prices.

I woke up half an hour out of Zhaoqing just as the China the mind's eye likes best, but is not always fooled by, was moving into the picture. Bicycles breezed along the tracks at the top of the river bank against a backdrop of misty mountains, banana plantations, water buffalo and small vegetable plots. Red-cheeked women bent over with the weight of the load across their shoulders appeared on the makeshift jetties at the water's edge. Rarely encountered in Guangdong, this was the quaint, rural China you see on ink scrolls. Arriving at the dock after a four-hour rather than the five-hour journey I had anticipated, there was great rejoicing in my private little heaven. The banks were high and there was a steep walk up forty-five steps to reach the terminal, a real struggle if you were arriving home from Hong Kong with heavy bags. At the top, passport control was disordered in a small-town kind of way. Arrival cards seemed to be on ration, and hordes of people were looking this way and that for their families, their luggage, the correct queue. Confusion reigned amidst those hundreds of people, but that's China, or at least that's one expectation of China. In fact all queues seemed to be the same though someone in a uniform came over and said: 'This way please,' and all foreign-

Chapter 6: Zhaoqing, the scenic spot

passport holders were subsequently shown to the front of the queue. Very nice, and not very China, at least not to my mind.

The ugly compound outside the terminal was full of rickety old buses, shabby mini-vans, and groups of people apparently just hanging around. A taxi driver, or rather a mini-van driver because this city has no taxis, pounced on me to the entertainment of the people hanging around and found his way on my behalf to the downtown Dynasty Hotel as requested. The meter looked like something from the ark and the driver wasn't even bothering to try to get it to work. Arriving he asked — in Cantonese — for RMB50. After a return comment — in Cantonese — that this seemed a tad expensive, he rapidly accepted RMB15. Bargaining for taxis and potentially getting ripped off every time unless you have specific local and language skills: very China, I thought. This trip was clearly not going to be all misty mountains and dewy eyes.

No I didn't have a reservation but yes they did have a vacant room. Up in the room, the bell boy who spoke the best English of anyone in the hotel turned the air conditioning down without prompt, personally called down to order up an adapter plug for a computer, and switched the television again without prompt straight to Hong Kong's TVB channel (relayed illegally in China, apparently) and a programme showing live footage of the Oscars. After all those misty mountains and pretty girls on bicycles, this city, according to expectations, was supposed to be an ultimate China experience. But here I was in a clean and cavernous hotel room costing less than RMB500 with a minibar and a television beaming out the extravagances of Hollywood.

Zhaoqing, situated on the banks of the Xi Jiang River in the northwest of Guangdong, is the province's most beautiful city. In the greater part of Guangdong, once-attractive landscapes of gentle hills and lively green paddy fields have all but disappeared to make way for modern factories and high-rise apartment blocks, and the major contemporary interest is not the cleanliness of the river but the interaction of communist politics and market economics. You can

Star Lake, Zhaoqing

Chapter 6: Zhaoqing, the scenic spot 131

even drop politics out of the equation, so little relevance does it seem to have to the lives of young working people, and just register supply and demand. Zhaoqing is a part of a province which most business travellers moving between SEZs and industrial zones could not imagine still exists. People in China are familiar with its discreet charms and natural beauty, tour groups from Taiwan, Hong Kong and Macau hosted by the local branch of China Travel arrive for two-day stays, but the place attracts scant tourists beyond Greater China. This state of affairs stands in sharp contrast to Guilin in Guangxi Province, some fifteen hours of driving from Zhaoqing and problematic to access except via the airport, which in spite of the demands of travel logistics manages to make it onto the typical around-the-world-in-a-year backpacker's itinerary. Or to Hangzhou in Jiangsu Province, site of the beautiful, weeping-willow-fringed West Lake which also attracts tourists from all over the world.

Zhaoqing the city nestles on the shore of the gently rippling Star Lake and the limestone Seven Star Crags which rise out of it. A two-minute walk from downtown, through the colourful arch, and you the observer become part of this beautiful vision of southern China which is almost enhanced by seasonal grey skies and light drizzle. Few landscapes improve in such weather conditions, but China's lakes and mountains take on a mysterious, greying beauty when the sky clouds over. Trees seem to grow straight out of the water, the lake is punctuated by little islands with pavilions accessed by quaint little bridges, and pretty temples are sheltered by trees at the peak of the crags. Roots of trees wind their way round ancient limestone rocks, and inside a cave Song dynasty calligraphy poetically extolling the beauty of Zhaoqing is picked out with coloured lights.

Star Lake is famed for combining Hangzhou's water and Guilin's hills (the lake is actually larger than West Lake though its crags are less numerous) and among Zhaoqing's other claims to fame such as lotus root, purple-back pelargonium tea and straw mats, fish from the Xi Jiang River and the reed-wrapped rice and bean dish called *guozheng*, come ink slabs. They can be readily purchased from in and around the temple and shops around Star Lake, some of them possessing considerable age and beauty. It is fascinating to speculate as to why this city should have spawned such a specialist industry. It is obvious that ink and misty mountain landscapes are made for each other. Mountains inspire the artist while ink allows them to render those mountains with a special ambience which would elude someone working in watercolours or oils.

Twenty minutes by car outside the city is the area's other most profoundly beautiful spot. Get successfully past the souvenir stalls and van drivers clamouring for business, and all that can be heard is leaves rustling, birds singing and water rushing over rocks and landing in pools below. Dinghu Mountain is what everyone would love China to be: a quiet spot with cool, clean air and lushly exotic subtropical plants and wildlife. More than 2,000 different kinds of tree grow up and down the peaks here, there are literally hundreds of different kinds of bird, snakes of every variety, as well as wild monkeys and wild chickens which appear or not depending on the volume of tourists visiting at any one time. Dozens of Chinese leaders, artists and intellectuals are said to have come to the mountain for inspiration. Dr Sun Yat Sen, who was born some miles south, visited with his wife in 1917 and, on a rock face at the base of the largest waterfall with a large pool beneath, the fact that he swam in these very waters is inscribed in beautiful red calligraphy in his wife's hand. The mountain's ecological significance is confirmed by UNESCO's presence here: one section remains closed to the public, reserved for research work. Special permission may be granted to parties such as school groups and apparently, from those who have been fortunate enough to get such permission, the area is marvellously rich in flora and fauna, untouched by man in the way of smart steps and resting arbours initiated for the comfort of visiting tourists.

Half-way up the mountain is the 400-year-old Qin Yun Temple, a three-storey affair with attractively decorative roofs and a 'cooking' area with a huge bowl known literally as the 'thousand pot', a reference to the fact that it could cook rice for 1,000 people at a time. Three smaller pots were used for cooking different vegetarian dishes each day. It is some indication of the religious importance of the temple

Chapter 6: Zhaoqing, the scenic spot

that up to 1,000 monks resided there. But what is most appealing about the temple, constantly visited by people burning joss sticks and bowing to the gold Buddhas, is the environment. While many of China's most beautiful temples are today defined by shabby tenements and ugly high-rises, look in any direction from Qin Yun and all you can see are forested mountain slopes. It really is exquisite.

That the area attracts few tourists from outside the region is not difficult to understand. It is now possible to travel to the city by train or boat from Hong Kong, or by road to Gongbei which is five minutes from Macau. There are two new four-star properties, Dynasty Hotel and Star Lake Hotel. But the tourism infrastructure effectively begins and ends with transport options and two hotels trying to approach international standard. The expanses of Star Lake make it suitable for canoeing, and Olympic-standard canoe training and dragon boat races are held there; the city also boasts the largest sports stadium in Guangdong Province outside Guangzhou. These amount to national rather than international attractions, however. The development of the exclusive Zhaoqing Resort & Golf Club with considerable Hong Kong backing and membership, the largest and probably most scenic course in China, has naturally brought more people to the city. But many own houses within the complex, they eat and entertain at the Club House, and rarely even visit the city.

Zhaoqing is essentially a poor and rural community; a city of considerable beauty where that beauty is, problematically, set against a backdrop of poverty one might not expect to experience in the Pearl River Delta region today. By the Rice Flowing Cave where legend says enough rice to feed the monk who looked after the temple appeared each morning from a small hole in a stone, a new statue in female form built of huge old stones pulled from the bottom of the cave presides over a series of new bridges, walkways and stepping stones, all intended to beautify the area still further. Yet minutes from the gateway to the cave, by the stop for the overcrowded N° 10 bus, young women were laughing together and gathering around a telephone, probably the only telephone in the village. They sat on wooden benches barely four inches wide and chewed on sugar cane. Makeshift restaurants with similarly proportioned benches and rickety tables geared up for the serving of a simple dinner, and someone got his hair cut by a street barber. Close by, women tended vegetable patches cultivated in the shadow of half-constructed buildings.

Zhaoqing City is betting on its so-called, appropriately called, 'scenic spots' but lacks the resources to develop its considerable natural assets and has little else to offer — to anyone. For young people, tourism offers the best career opportunities, but most students who go off to university in Guangzhou never return except to visit families. This means the city barely has a professional class, and the bulk of its citizens remain involved either in agriculture or work in huge state-owned factories producing bicycles, meters, magnets and cement.

The people who do choose to live there when they have a choice through education to leave, love the quality of life, however. Motivations and even beliefs are surely influenced if not shaped by the environments in which we live, and while it might sound romantic to imagine that the Cantonese who live in Zhaoqing are more interested in their souls than their wallets, there are some extraordinary people in the city. People who regret the surge of motorbikes in the city ('almost one per household,' said one bicycle owner in horror, guessing that means there are around 50,000 on the roads) and people who are living their own lives free from the demands of society with regard to, for example, marriage.

Shi Min, the manager of one of the local hotels, is the cousin of a friend of mine in Hong Kong. She is also a divorcee, but there's little hint of internal turmoil about this domestic arrangement. Financially independent with a large car which goes with the job, a mobile phone and a pager, she takes care of her ten-year-old son who is apparently brilliant both academically and in sports. She can afford to eat in good restaurants, and relishes that. She knows about all the local dishes, traditional and otherwise, and orders a fantastic seafood lunch at one of the city's top restaurants; a generous and perfect hostess. The venue she selected was a restaurant out on the water. Not the tourist trap of

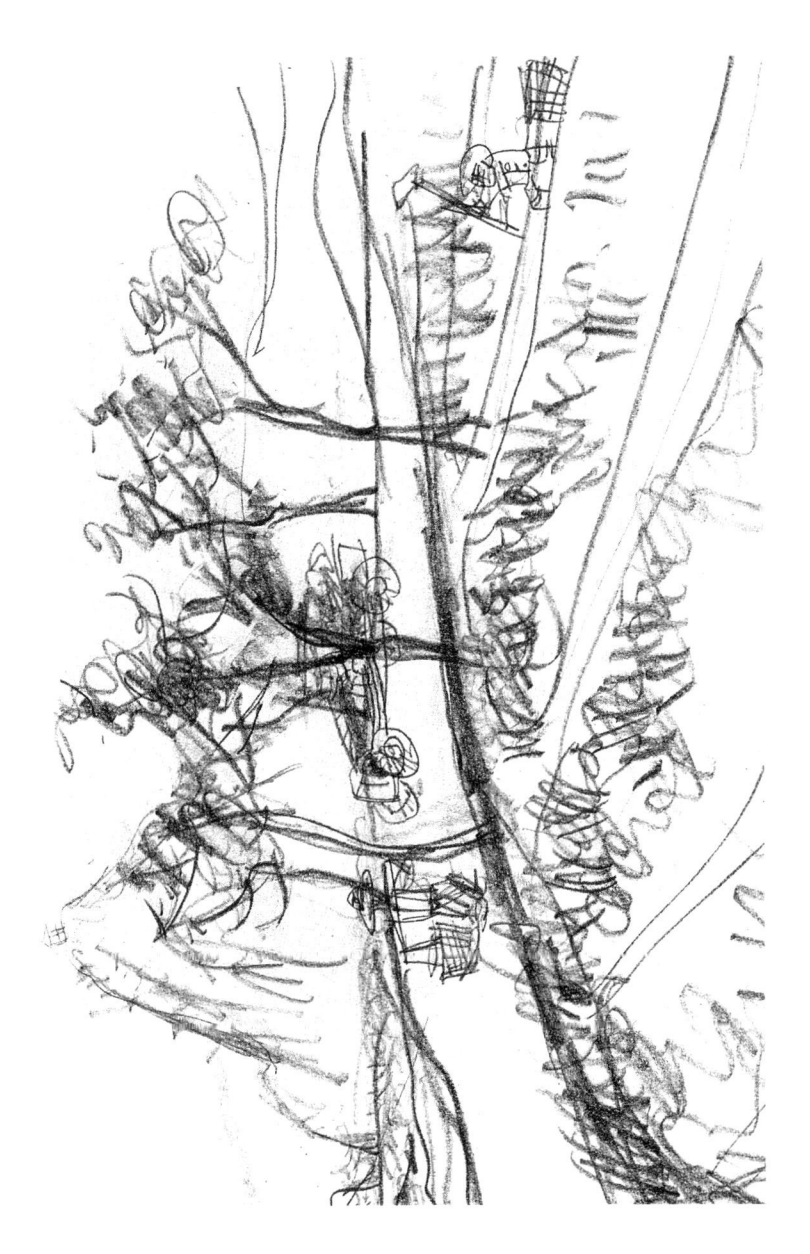

Rural road, Zhaoqing

Hong Kong's Floating Restaurant in Aberdeen but a place which offers some of the freshest fish available, much of which is unique to the Xi Jiang river.

Her bubbly assistant, Elaine Chan, and my designated guide, took the unusual decision to move to Zhaoqing a year ago after graduating from a university in Guangzhou, although her parents live two hours away. Clearly a kindred spirit with Shi Min, she lives alone, still extremely unusual in China. She loves to eat though she worries about her weight, she reads in the evening, she walks up Dinghu Mountain on the weekend, and visits her father, a government official, about once a month. As for the cyanide problem which had threatened to abort my trip, she said she had heard something vague about it when I queried the extent of the problem. 'Has anyone died?' I asked. 'We wouldn't hear,' she told me.

Out for lunch together — Elaine said her boss is fantastic and the combination of a happy working life and a clean city was as much as she could wish for — you couldn't meet more fun-loving and contented women. They may be exceptional, but the population at large does not appear discontented. People understand they could earn more than the average RMB800 per month if they moved to Foshan or Zhongshan, but they love the quiet beauty of their home city. Some regret that the government seems to take a rather passive role in development when compared with the officials in other cities in the province, and indeed it does seem that prosperity or otherwise in the Pearl River Delta is today measured in direct proportion to the dynamism of the leadership. Some residents socialise for a beer or go to *karaoke* bars at night, but pastimes tend to be more simple: reading, watching television and, on the weekends, visiting their 'scenic spots' for some exercise in the freshest of air. Zhaoqing residents are immensely proud of these spots. Praise a scenic spot and it is as if you are praising them personally. 'Thank you, thank you,' they'll say. 'Thank you.'

The journey by road from Zhaoqing down towards Zhuhai provided more landscapes one imagines have been forever lost in China and which are more likely to appear in Vietnam or Cambodia — expanses

Chapter 6: Zhaoqing, the scenic spot 137

of paddy fields or terraces dotted with the bent bodies of farmers, all framed by forested hills and divided up by little rivers. Instead of the two-storey white brick homes with roof space which typify the landscape further south, here houses were more often one-storey and made of recycled red bricks. They might be less than five years old but because of the age of the bricks they looked far more mature than their years and low construction skills have resulted in warped walls and caving-in roofs which also suggest they have been there decades.

Pay double and you can do this journey down through Foshan and Zhongshan in a non-stop, twenty-seat minibus. These non-stop buses, said Zhaoqing tour guides, are not allowed to stop, so they're very safe. Less than thirty seconds from the bus station what happened? The bus stopped. Or rather, it paused briefly, so briefly it could barely be accused of stopping, but long enough to pick up a customer. 'Quickly, quickly,' said the bus conductor as he relayed the price of a ticket. At keenly located bus-stops he leant out of the window: 'Zhongshan, Zhuhai, Gongbei,' he called. Sometimes he hopped off the bus to encourage more passengers to step aboard but the delay sometimes made the driver nervous. The two were colluding in a sensitively-conceived operation to maximise profits on this four-hour route, but stop for a second too long and fines or, worse, the loss of an operating licence, could result. Indeed, once or twice the bus pulled into a stop when the driver suddenly spotted a police car 100 metres down the road. He quickly moved the bus on. Sometimes passengers were not allowed to disembark where they wanted to for similar security reasons.

The mastermind behind this operation was the slickly attractive bus conductor who negotiated prices and held all the money he made in his left hand, stroking it with his right. He couldn't let it out of his sight. The efforts he put into encouraging more custom were exemplary and certainly suggested he came not from Zhaoqing but from go-ahead Zhuhai. Down there, the Cantonese understand that if you put in that extra effort you make that extra buck. Put in that extra effort a few times a day and you make quite a few extra bucks. And bucks create bucks. He helped customers on and off the bus, lifting bags and pulling down seats. He was a bit of showman, chatting and laughing with customers and smiling at the girls; he was a clever and witty conversationalist as quick in mind as he was with his arms as he shut the bus door to escape the attention of a passing police motorcycle.

He admitted no robbers, not even anyone who had as much as an unattractive glint in the eye. Unless he was in a very clever commission operation whereby he would let his own money be stolen in a pretend raid from which he would reap a percentage of the proceeds, he was unlikely to risk losing all his hard-earned money. He obviously knew when to stop the bus and when not to; who was a genuine cash-carrying customer and who simply wanted to get his hands on someone else's notes. At Gongbei, the crossing point between Macau and Zhuhai, he carried bags off the bus and slipping into Mandarin for the first time, presumably according to his observation that more foreigners understand Mandarin than Cantonese, kindly told me where the border gate was. He sat down for a beer.

I picked up a duty-free bottle of what promised to be an excellent red Burgundy and walked back into Macau.

About the author

Brought up on a farm in the Sussex countryside, Annabel Jackson graduated in English Literature and, after moving to Hong Kong in 1989, worked for *Hong Kong Tatler* and the *South China Morning Post* before turning freelance to work for a number of Asia-Pacific and international publications. She is now director of public relations at the Mandarin Oriental, Hong Kong hotel.

Best known in Asia for her idiosyncratic food and wine writing, she has published three food/culture books: *Macau on a Plate* (Roundhouse Publications, 1994), *Vietnam on a Plate* (Roundhouse Publications, 1996) and *Street Café Vietnam* (Conran Octopus, 1998), and is now working on a Macanese cookbook.

Farewell My Colony
by Todd Crowell

A journal of the final two years of Hong Kong under British rule, by a American writer and long-term Hong Kong resident Todd Crowell. He joined politicians seeking votes in the elections under Governor Patten's last-minute attempt to install a democratic tradition, and reports on the "selection" of a rival legislature and of shipping magnate Tung Chee-hwa as the first Chinese leader of the territory. He tells how Hong Kong's Chinese and expatriates, *taipan*s and cagemen, come to terms with the impending change of sovereignty.

"An intelligent and illuminating book, the stylish writing is itself a source of pleasure . . . scores some palpable hits on the prediction front. An excellent acquisition for anyone who needs a briefing on recent Hong Kong history."
— *Asiaweek*

ISBN 962-7160-54-7

Hong Kong Pathfinder
by Martin Williams

Martin Williams leads you on 21 day-trips in Hong Kong. Following his steps, you will explore rugged hills, forested valleys, reservoirs and waterfalls, temples and aging villages, long-abandoned forts and near-uninhabited islands.

"Williams' book is small, attractively bound, and includes a good selection of unusual photos taken by the author. It gives good coverage, including six walks on outer islands, 10 in the New Territories, and two on Hong Kong Island. The walks vary in length from 3 to 15km, so the book is suitable for everyone and all seasons, and should appeal to residents and tourists alike."
— *Hong Kong Birdwatching Society Bulletin*

"Thoughtful and meticulously researched"   — *Action Asia Magazine*

"A boon for neophyte ramblers in Hong Kong and a handy reference for old hiking hands."
— *Discovery*

ISBN 962-7160-72-5 (fourth revised edition), with 23 maps, 15 photos

Cantonese Culture

Aspects of life in modern Hong Kong and Southeast Asia
Shirley Ingram & Rebecca S Y Ng

A guide to the etiquette and customs of Hong Kong and other Southeast Asian cities. Separated from the mainland, the Cantonese of southern China have preserved many Chinese traditions lost in China, adapting them to their lives in the modern metropolises of Asia and the Chinatowns of Western countries.

The rituals of daily life — birth, death, marriage, and the many festivals that make up the Chinese calendar are described and explained. Every visitor or long-term resident will find this book invaluable.

ISBN 962-7160-37-7

Getting Along With the Chinese

for fun and profit
by Fred Schneiter

The best-selling entertaining and highly informative guide to working and playing with the Chinese.

Schneiter delves into the lighter side of Chinese psychology and demystifies one of the toughest markets in the world. He explains when you should and how you can apply pressure, why patience is not quite the overriding consideration it is generally perceived to be, and what to do and what not to do when hosting Chinese guests.

"An essential item to pack in your 'China survival kit'"
— *The Hongkong Standard*

"Facts on China no degree of study can give" — *The Shanghai Star*

"Everyone working with Chinese, in or out of China, should read this and send a copy to their boss!" — **Daniel Ng, McDonald's South China**

"An insightful book that will help those traveling to China and enlighten anyone intrigued by cross-cultural relations." — *The Oregonian*

ISBN 962-7160-19-9

Walking to the Mountain
by Wendy Teasdill

This is the story of a journey made on foot across Tibet to Mount Kailash. Kailash has been attracting pilgrims of all religions for thousands of years, but until recently only a handful of Westerners had ever been there.

"Wendy Teasdill provides a vivid personal account of how she was drawn to Mount Kailash. Inspired by the beauty of the landscape and her admiration for the Tibetan people she met, she reached her goal."
— **The Dalai Lama**

"A testament to courage and commitment. Its style is crisp, poignant and quietly stirring. The narrative has the steady pounding beat of the lone trekker with a mission." — *Asiaweek*

ISBN 962-7160-27-x

Red Chips
and the globalisation of China's enterprises
by Charles de Trenck, Simon Cartledge, Anil Daswani, David Sakmar, Christian A. Katz

Ground-breaking analysis of the real assets and structures behind the "Red Chip" Chinese companies as they join the international stock market, by a team of Hong Kong financial analysts.

"Thought to be the first of its kind, *Red Chips* deals with the history of the corporatisation process on the mainland. Chapters are devoted to such prototypes as Citic Beijing and Citic Pacific, and other leading companies. It deals with the complex structures around which listed entities are formed and operate, and focuses on the links to the state banking sector."
— *South China Morning Post*

"*Red Chips* provides enough in the way of facts and figures to be a useful resource for anyone seeking to find out about the structures and operations of China's conglomerates." — *Finance Asia*

ISBN 962-7160-64-4 (second revised edition)

Cheung Chau Dog Fanciers' Society by Alan B Pierce

"An accurate slice of Hong Kong life — touching on heroin smuggling, money laundering, corruption in the police force as well as in one of Hong Kong's most wealthy and powerful Chinese families — but it also depicts a very local journey of self-discovery. A superb description of insular life, complete with beery expatriates, ploddish village policemen, arm-wrestling triads and masses of day-trippers. A thriller with a difference."
— *Hongkong Standard*

"One of the best Hong Kong novels ever written. It puts James Clavell to shame." — *HK Magazine*

ISBN 962-7160-38-5

Temutma by Rebecca Bradley and John Stewart Sloan

Temutma, a *kuang-shi,* a monster similar to the vampire of European legend, is imprisoned beneath Kowloon Walled City in Hong Kong by his ancient keeper, until it escapes....

"Page-turning... intelligent writing and suspense, suspense, suspense... thrilling" — *South China Morning Post*

ISBN 962-7160-47-4

Hong Kong Rose by Xu Xi

From a crumbling perch with a view of the Statue of Liberty, Rose Kho, Hong Kong girl who made it, lost it, and may be about to make it or lose it again, reflects, scotch in hand, on a life that "like an Indonesian mosquito disrupting my Chinese sleep" has controls of its own.

ISBN 962-7160-55-5

Riding a Tiger by Robert Abel

"A lively, upbeat and humorous look at Beijing life through the eyes of an unabashed Westerner." — *South China Morning Post*

ISBN 962-7160-50-4

Chinese Opera by Alex Kuo

"An American goes to his ancestral land, China, and confronts the strangenesses there. What life after revolution? After many revolutions? Alex Kuo helps us hear the music that strangers play to strangers, and a free individual plays to society." — **Maxine Hong Kingston**

"Kuo gave himself an ambitious task, setting his story of an American-Chinese exploring his cultural roots against one of the most vivid historical backdrops of the century." — *South China Morning Post*

ISBN 962-7160-59-8

Other titles from Asia 2000

Non-fiction

Cantonese Culture	Shirley Ingram & Rebecca Ng
Concise World Atlas	Maps International
Egg Woman's Daughter	Mary Chan
Farewell, My Colony	Todd Crowell
Getting Along With the Chinese	Fred Schneiter
Hong Kong Pathfinder	Martin Williams
Korean Dynasty — Hyundai and Chung Ju Yung	Donald Kirk
Red Chips and the Globalisation of China's Enterprises	Charles de Trenck
The Rise & Decline of the Asian Century	Christopher Lingle
Walking to the Mountain	Wendy Teasdill

Fiction

Cheung Chau Dog Fanciers' Society	Alan B Pierce
Chinese Opera	Alex Kuo
Daughters of Hui	Xu Xi (Sussy Chakó)
Getting to Lamma	Jan Alexander
Hong Kong Rose	Xu Xi (Sussy Chakó)
Riding a Tiger	Robert Abel
Temutma	Rebecca Bradley & Stewart Sloan

Poetry

An Amorphous Melody	Kavita
New Ends, Old Beginnings	Louise Ho
Round — Poems and Photographs of Asia	Madeleine Slavick & Barbara Baker
Travelling with a Bitter Melon	Leung Ping-kwan
Woman to Woman and other poems	Agnes Lam

Order from Asia 2000 Ltd
302 Seabird House, 22–28 Wyndham St
Central, Hong Kong
tel (852) 2530-1409; fax (852) 2526-1107
email sales@asia2000.com.hk; http://www.asia2000.com.hk/

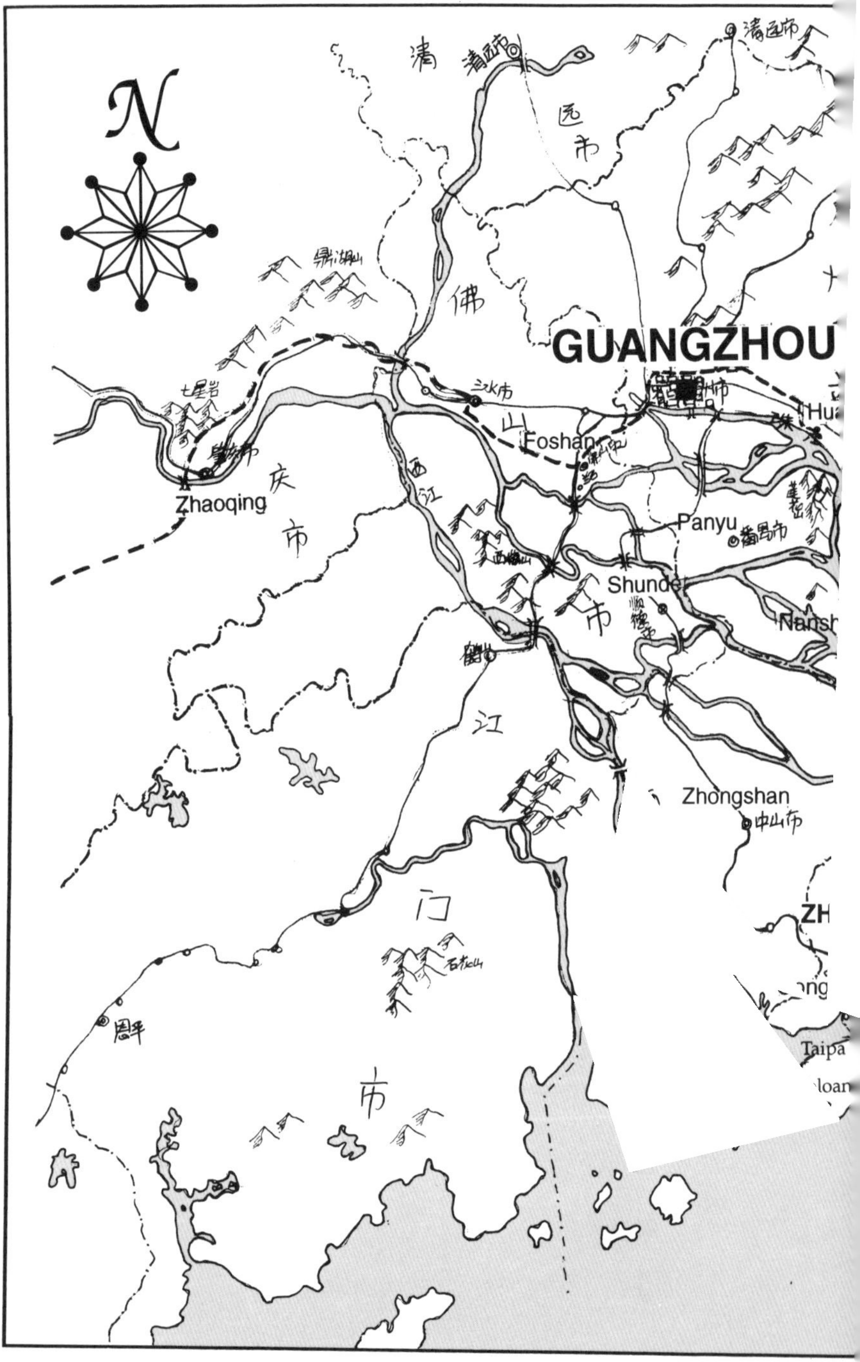
N
清
清远市
远
市
佛
GUANGZHOU
三水市
山
Foshan
Zhaoqing
庆
市
西
江
Panyu
番禺市
Shunde
顺德市
市
江
Zhongshan
中山市
门
石花山
恩平
市
Taipa